JUSTIN GAU
3, PUMP COURT
TEMPLE
LONDON EC4
0171-353 0711
524 344 955
1989

ENGLISH
CANON LAW

ERIC WALDRAM KEMP

ENGLISH
CANON LAW

Essays in Honour of Bishop Eric Kemp

Edited by

NORMAN DOE
MARK HILL
ROBERT OMBRES

UNIVERSITY OF WALES PRESS
CARDIFF
1998

© The Contributors, 1998

British Library Cataloguing-in-Publication Data.
A catalogue record for this book is available from the British Library.

ISBN 0–7083–1478–3

Typeset at University of Wales Press and Gwasg Dinefwr
Printed in Great Britain by Gwasg Dinefwr, Llandybïe

Contents

Foreword

Few other bishops this century can have celebrated the silver jubilee of their consecration whilst still in office, in the same see. Yet, next year marks the twenty-fifth anniversary of Eric Kemp's consecration by Michael Ramsey and his enthronement as the 102nd Bishop of Chichester. He brought to the bench of bishops a sharp intellect and clearly defined sense of purpose and to the diocese real pastoral care coupled with firm discipline which many have deeply appreciated down the years.

It is therefore timely that he be honoured in this book of essays. For Eric is not merely a spirited bishop, but he is also a distinguished historian, theologian, ecumenist and canonist. I am therefore delighted that the essays in this volume mirror his various interests and achievements and contribute to the present renaissance in the study of the laws of the church. Such a renaissance would have been impossible had Eric's still small voice not been heard on commissions, committees and, not least, the Court of Ecclesiastical Causes Reserved, over many decades.

But perhaps his most lasting achievement has been to foster and inform the dialogue between the church and her lawyers. As President of the Ecclesiastical Law Society since its foundation in 1987, Eric has encouraged a vibrant discussion of canon law and the secular law as it affects the church. He may not agree with all of the opinions expressed in the papers in this volume. But no stranger to controversy himself, I anticipate he will enjoy the stimulus of debate.

This volume represents a critical examination of our current understanding of English canon law, its history and ecclesiology and its relationship with secular law. It is a fitting and lasting tribute to the scholarship, ministry and tenacity of Bishop Eric Kemp.

+ George Cantuar
Lambeth Palace, SE1

Editorial Preface

The silver jubilee of the consecration of the Right Reverend Eric Kemp as Bishop of Chichester which falls in 1999 will be marked in many ways and by many people. The eve of this anniversary is a timely occasion upon which to recall Bishop Kemp's immense contribution to both the study and the administration of canon law in the Church of England. The timing of this tribute is also a reflection of the wider appeal enjoyed by canon law during recent years. The formation of the Ecclesiastical Law Society in 1987 was largely due to the determination of Bishop Kemp and, as president since its inception, he has ensured that it has flourished as a vital – and occasionally vocal – grouping of clergy and lawyers. As Bishop Kemp himself stated in a paper delivered at the Society's inaugural conference, 'the law of the church cannot be properly understood and properly administered without something more than a perfunctory knowledge of theology and church history'.

Born on 27 April 1915, Eric Waldram Kemp was educated at Brigg Grammar School, Lincolnshire and Exeter College and St Stephen's House, Oxford. Ordained deacon in 1939 and priest in 1940, he served his title at St Luke's Church, Southampton, returning to Oxford in 1941 as librarian of Pusey House and, subsequently, as fellow, chaplain, tutor and lecturer in theology and medieval history at Exeter College, obtaining a doctorate of divinity in 1961. In 1969 he was appointed Dean of Worcester and was a regular member of the Convocation of Canterbury, the Church Assembly and, in due course, General Synod. Amongst other appointments held have been canon and prebendary of Caistor in Lincoln Cathedral (from 1952), honorary provincial canon of Cape Town (from 1960) and chaplain to the Queen (1967–9). In 1974 he was appointed Bishop of Chichester. He

chaired the Faculty Jurisdiction Commission whose recommendations in the report *The Continuing Care of Churches and
Cathedrals* (1983) have largely been implemented in legislative form.

There is about Bishop Kemp himself something of a characteristic modesty and quietness of spirit. He is rooted in the best
traditions of the English church and at home in its institutions. He
has much of the spirit, temper and learning of the Caroline Divines
and of the Tractarians. He is a convocation man *par excellence*,
less at ease in General Synod though none the less sure-footed
there. The public impression is of ruminative calm and unfussiness.
There is steel in him and there have been public occasions – an
early Catholic Renewal Conference springs to mind – where an
audience has been aroused by the sheer passion of his advocacy.
Bishop Kemp has always been his own man and has known his own
mind, even if the result has been occasional unpopularity. Not
many now remember that the then Dean of Worcester was for a
period in the 1960s and early 1970s out of favour with those who
then ran the Church Union because he aligned himself with Archbishop Michael Ramsey's vigorous advocacy of the Anglican-
Methodist unity scheme.

The purpose of this collection of essays is twofold. Primarily it is
a tribute to a man whose contribution to the study and teaching of
the canon law of England this century is unique. Its renaissance in
recent years as a distinct discipline is largely due to the tireless and
– until now – somewhat unacknowledged work of Bishop Kemp.
As historian, theologian and priest, he has continuously sought to
keep alive the work and achievement of earlier canonists. As
bishop, he became and remains a legislator and enforcer of the law
– benign but resolute. Secondly, however, in the climate of debate
and discussion fostered by Bishop Kemp, this volume seeks to make
a contribution to the critical analysis of the laws of the church at
the end of the second millennium. By bringing together specialists
in the field of the history, ecclesiology and current operation of the
church's laws, it is hoped to stimulate an informed appraisal of the
canon law of England as it has been, as it is now and as it may,
perhaps, become.

From the bibliography of Bishop Kemp's main publications
which follows, certain abiding themes emerge: the nature and
history of canon law; the structures and laws of the Church
of England; ecumenism; worship and theology. In inviting

contributions for this volume we chose established authors whose work complements and takes forward the major underlying themes in the writings of Bishop Kemp. The first four chapters emphasize history, the next four are more explicitly theological, and the last four deal with substantive aspects of contemporary English canon law.

Dr Evans and Monsignor Ferme guide us through the medieval canon law of England, both cosmopolitan and local. Professor Helmholz and Professor Bray consider some of the effects of the Reformation on the established patterns of legislation and interpretation. Fr Ombres and Bishop Hill examine how the drive for ecumenical convergence affects canon law and the understanding of ordained ministry, particularly that of bishops. Chancellor Bursell explores certain aspects of law concerning liturgical matters. The Reverend T. G. Watkin views the relation of church and state in a long perspective. In terms of contemporary canon law, Dr Doe analyses the different ways adopted by the Church of England when it comes to regulating its internal life and governance, whilst Mr Hill explores the increasing supervision of church courts by the civil courts. Mr Harte considers how the law treats religious education and worship in state schools. Finally, Chancellor McClean's paper on establishment in a European context indicates the dimension in which English canon law will increasingly be considered. This concluding chapter echoes the opening one which begins with the reflection that the Norman Conquest brought England into the European legal system more decisively than her entry into the European Community was able to do until the late 1990s.

The editors would like to express their thanks to the Ecclesiastical Law Society for its support of this venture, which was first suggested by Robert Ombres, and to the Reverend Sir Derek Pattinson for his assistance with the writing of this preface. Particular thanks are also due to the contributors, each of whom took up the invitation to write without demur but with enthusiasm and goodwill undaunted by the strict and relentless demands of the editors. The library of Pusey House, Oxford, and its staff along with its former librarian, Bishop Kemp himself, were invaluable in the search for references to various publications in a compendious bibliography spanning six decades. Without the generous support of a visiting fellowship at Emmanuel College, Cambridge, Mark

Hill would have been unable to procure and collate the various contributions, still less pen his own. Finally, the subscribers whose names appear towards the end of this volume are to be thanked. Their number and diversity is, in itself, no small tribute to Bishop Kemp in whose honour we are pleased and proud to present this *festschrift*.

Norman Doe, Cardiff
Mark Hill, Cambridge
Robert Ombres, Oxford

Feast of the Ascension, 1998

Bibliography
of the Main Publications of
Bishop Eric Kemp

ROBERT OMBRES

1937 'The Augustinian Tradition in the Religious Life', *Church Quarterly Review*, 125 (1937), pp.19–47.

1943 'The Discipline of the Church: Canon Law and the Ecclesiastical Courts', in *Thy Household the Church: Proposals for Government and Order in the Church of England*, by a Group of the Clergy (Westminster, 1943), pp.37–53.

'Reconstruction in the Church of England', *Agenda* (1943), reprinted as No.1 of the *Church and Realm* series published by the Church Literature Association.

1945 'Pope Alexander III and the Canonization of the Saints', *Transactions of the Royal Historical Society*, 4th series, 27 (1945), pp.13–28.

1946 'Zeger Bernhard Van Espen', *Theology*, 49 (1946), pp.194–200, 227–32.

1947 'Legal Reform in the Church of England', *Illuminatio*, 1 (1947), pp.29–33.

1948 *Canonization and Authority in the Western Church* (Oxford, 1948).

E. G. Wood, *The Regal Power of the Church: or, the Fundamentals of the Canon Law* (Cambridge, 1888), with a

Preface and a Supplementary Bibliography by E. W. Kemp (Westminster, 1948).

Canon Law in the Church of England. Church Literature Association of the Church Union (London, [*c*.1948]).

1950   'Das Buch of Common Prayer', *Internationale Kirchliche Zeitschrift*, 40 (1950), pp.39–46.

1952   'The Origins of the Canterbury Convocation', *The Journal of Ecclesiastical History*, 3 (1952), pp.132–43.

1953   'Laity in Church Government', *Parson and Parish*, 17 (1953), pp.31–2.

'Round Table Conference', *Parson and Parish*, 20 (1953), pp.10–11.

'The Roman Catholic Doctrine of Marriage', *Theology*, 56 (1953), pp.251–5.

1954   *Papal Decretals Relating to the Diocese of Lincoln in the Twelfth Century*, ed. W. Holtzmann and E. W. Kemp, The Lincoln Record Society, 47 (Hereford, 1954).

'The Canterbury Convocation', *Parson and Parish*, 22 (1954), pp.4–6.

N. P. Williams (London, 1954).

1955   'The Attempted Canonization of Robert Grosseteste', in D. A. Callus (ed.), *Robert Grosseteste* (Oxford, 1955), Appendix 2, pp.241–6.

K. E. Kirk, *Beauty and Bands, and Other Papers*, prepared by E. W. Kemp (London, 1955).

'Bishops and Presbyters at Alexandria', *The Journal of Ecclesiastical History*, 6 (1955), pp.125–42.

1957   *An Introduction to Canon Law in the Church of England*, being the Lichfield Cathedral Divinity Lectures for 1956 (London, 1957).

'Apostolic Succession', *Faith and Unity*, 4 (1957), pp.3–7.

1959 *The Life and Letters of Kenneth Escott Kirk, Bishop of Oxford 1937–1954* (London, 1959).

1961 *Counsel and Consent: Aspects of the Government of the Church as Exemplified in the History of the English Provincial Synods*, The Bampton Lectures for 1960 (London, 1961).

1964 *The Anglican-Methodist Conversations: A Comment from Within* (London, 1964).

1965 'The Canterbury Provincial Chapter and the Collegiality of Bishops in the Middle Ages', in *Études d'histoire du droit canonique dédiées à Gabriel Le Bras* (Paris, 1965), vol. 1, pp.185–94.

1966 'The Anglican–Methodist Conversations', *Internationale Kirchliche Zeitschrift*, 56 (1966), pp.200–8.

1967 'The Church of England and the Old Catholic Churches', in E. G. W. Bill (ed.), *Anglican Initiatives in Christian Unity* (London, 1967), pp.145–62.

1968 'Anglican Orders', *One in Christ*, 4 (1968), pp.380–2.

1969 'Die Anglikanisch-Methodistische Unionsplan', *Internationale Kirchliche Zeitschrift*, 59 (1969), pp.126–33.

'Augustinianism', in E. W. Kemp (ed.), *Man: Fallen and Free. Oxford Essays on the Condition of Man* (London, 1969), pp.158–71.

The Anglican–Methodist Unity Scheme, published with F. Colquhoun, *Evangelicals and Methodist Unity* (Windsor, 1969), pp.1–22.

1970 'Das Primatsverständnis in der Anglikanischen Theologie', *Internationale Kirchliche Zeitschrift*, 60 (1970), pp.385–93.

1974 'The Organization of the English Episcopate from the Reformation to the Twentieth Century', *Aspects de l'Anglicanisme*, Colloque de Strasbourg, 14–16 June 1972 (Paris, 1974), pp. 25–38.

1976 *Inaugural Address to the General Council of the Church Union as President*, Church Union (London, 1976).

1977 'Jubilee – Jollification and Holiness', *The Server*, 10 (1977), pp.11–13.

'The Art of Worship', *The Occasional Journal of the Alcuin Club* (1977), pp.1–7.

1980 *Square Words in a Round World* (Glasgow, 1980).

'The Structure of Theology', Birmingham Additional Curates Society, *Kairos*, 2 (1980), pp.9–14.

1981 *Milk Without Guile: Address to the Deanery Synods of the Diocese of Chichester* (Chichester, 1981).

'History and Action in the Sermons of a Medieval Archbishop', in R. H. C. Davis and J. M. Wallace-Hadrill (eds.), *The Writing of History in the Middle Ages: Essays Presented to Richard William Southern* (Oxford, 1981), pp.349–65.

'Bonn Agreement Golden Jubilee Celebrations', *Internationale Kirchliche Zeitschrift*, 71 (1981), pp.223–30.

1982 'Mary and Right Belief in Christ', in A. Stacpoole (ed.), *Mary's Place in Christian Dialogue* (Slough, 1982), pp.63–78.

'Personal Memories', in C. Van Kasteel, P. J. Maan and M. F. G. Parmentier (eds.), *Kracht in Zwakheid van een Kleine Wereldkerk. De Oud-Katholieke Unie van Utrecht. Studie Aangeboden aan Marinus Kok, Aartsbisschop van Utrecht (1970–1981)* (Hilversum, 1982), pp.205–6.

1984 *Joy in Believing: Sermons Preached by the Lord Bishop of Chichester on the Occasion of the Tenth Anniversary of his Consecration* (Chichester, 1984).

1986 'The Creation of the Synod', in P. Moore (ed.), *The Synod of Westminster: Do We Need It?* (London, 1986), pp.10–24.

1987 'The Spirit of the Canon Law and its Application in England', *Ecclesiastical Law Journal*, 1 (1–2) (1987), pp.5–14.

1988 'The Problems of Church Relationships Facing the Anglican Communion in the Coming Lambeth Conference', *Internationale Kirchliche Zeitschrift*, 78 (1988), pp.65–78.

1989 'Legal Implications of Lambeth', *Ecclesiastical Law Journal*, 1 (5) (1989), pp.15–23.

1992 T. Briden and B. Hanson (eds.), *Moore's Introduction to English Canon Law*, with a Foreword by Bishop E. Kemp (3rd edn. London, 1992), pp.vii–viii.

'Fede, ordine e strutture ecclesiastiche nell'Anglicanesimo contemporaneo', in C. Alzati (ed.), *L'Anglicanesimo: Dalla Chiesa d'Inghilterra alla Comunione Anglicana* (Genoa, 1992), pp. 237–47.

1995 *The Bishop's Address to the Deanery Synods 1994–95* (Chichester, 1995).

1998 'Unity – Lessons to be Learned; Issues to be Faced: Anglican–Methodist Conversations 1956–1972', *Ecclesiastical Law Journal*, 5 (1998), pp.76–9.

1

Lanfranc, Anselm and a New Consciousness of Canon Law in England

GILLIAN EVANS

The Norman Conquest brought England into the European legal system more decisively than her entry in the European Community was able to do before the late 1990s. In Lanfranc (1070–89) she had an archbishop reared in Italy, probably possessing some legal training,[1] and experienced from his time at Bec and Caen in the legal problems which could arise for monasteries holding lands in northern France. His successor, Anselm (1093–1109), was an extremely reluctant administrator but he was forced in the course of his disputes with two kings of England to think out his legal position and his ideas about law. Anselm had a mind of a calibre which encouraged him to place the questions which arose in the largest possible intellectual context and, above all, to see them as in the first instance theological.

Sources and Systematization

The continental European scene of the Carolingian to eleventh-century periods had been marked by various attempts to compile lists of canons. The problem was that there was no corpus. It had to be created, out of canons of councils and decrees of popes, in circumstances where no one could say which councils' decrees were

---

[1] M. T. Gibson, *Lanfranc of Bec* (Oxford, 1978), pp.36–7, 139–40, depending a good deal on Z. N. Brooke, *The English Church and the Papacy* (Cambridge, 1952), pp.32–3 which remains a definitive study on the English scene.

universally binding and which had merely *local* authority. Anselm understood the rules of territoriality of episcopal jurisdiction. On William, bishop-elect of Winchester, Anselm writes to King Henry: the King had sent the bishop out of England; if he has thus sent him away, Anselm cannot consecrate him.[2]

Burchard of Worms made an early attempt to list and to systematize church law. But the divisions were pragmatically rather than theoretically conceived. He was interested, for example, in the powers and duties of bishops because those kept being called into question by events. About 1050 a collection in 74 titles was put together, in which can be perceived early stirrings of a centralizing tendency, in the greater emphasis on the role of the papacy in the government of the Church. By the era of Gregory VII (1073–85) that had become paramount.[3] Lanfranc's Letter 39 is to Pope Gregory VII. In it he recognizes his canonical subjection to the universal primate.[4]

Papal plenitude of power could, paradoxically, strengthen the position of other metropolitans. Lanfranc points in a letter to various canons, among other authorities, stressing the authority of the metropolitan.[5] Eadmer's narrative of 'recent events' has Anselm insisting that he cannot be metropolitan of the whole of Britain, since York's archbishop is metropolitan in his province; but he can be primate.[6]

England stood a little apart from the concerns of the rest of Europe in some respects, showing for some years little of the preoccupation with the debates of the eleventh century on simony and clerical marriage which were exercising lawyers and theologians on the continent. Gilbert Crispin, Anselm's pupil, produced two treatises on these subjects as abbot of Westminster, but that was well after the changes brought about by the Conquest

---

[2] Letter 265, *Anselmi Opera Omnia*, ed. F. S. Schmitt (Rome and Edinburgh, 1938–68), 6 vols., Vol.4, p.180: 'si illum expellitis de terra vestra, ut mihi non liceat eandem consecrationem canonice facere: videtur mihi quia dissaisitis me de officio meo, sine iudicio cur facere debeatis'.

[3] P. Fournier, *Les collections canoniques romaines de l'époque de Grégoire VII* (Paris, 1920).

[4] *The Letters of Lanfranc*, ed. H. Clover and M. Gibson (Oxford, 1979), pp.130–1: 'mens mea preceptis vestris in omnibus et per omnia secundum canonum praecepta subiaceat'.

[5] Ibid., pp.152–3: 'sunt alia plurima de excellentia et potestate primatum atque archiepiscoporum tam in prefatis scripturis tam in aliis orthodoxorum patrum auctenticis libris'.

[6] Eadmer, *Historia Novorum*, ed. M. Rule, Rolls Series (London, 1884), p.42.

had raised consciousness.[7] By that time England had moved its thinking steadily into the Continental frame.

A legatine council was held at Winchester in April 1070.[8] It has among its *capitula*: the insistence that no bishop may hold two sees (1), and that no one may be ordained by a simoniac (2), that priests are not to be received without letters of recommendation from their bishops (3), matters which had clearly been arising in practice, but which also raised crucial canon-law questions going to those areas of ecclesiology where faith and order meet. The canons of the council held at London in 1075 are fuller and more explicit about such connections. They cite a number of the canons.[9] By April 1076, when a primatial council was held at Winchester, the issue of clerical celibacy was coming first.[10] At the 1102 council at Westminster it is possible to see theory coming together with practice. First the council, basing itself on patristic authority, condemned simony as a heresy. There follows a list of persons found blameworthy *in qua culpa inventi*.[11] There is a similar condemnation of clerical marriage, with a sanction. The children of priests may not inherit their fathers' livings.[12]

There was not merely a new connectedness with the continent created by the Norman Conquest, and a concomitant heightened awareness of the legal framework and the legal implications of the practical problems which belonged within it. The character of the two archbishops was also transformative. There is no known copy of Burchard's *Decretals* in England in Lanfranc's time. The copy at Bec in the twelfth century does not tell us that it was there in Lanfranc's day.[13] But Lanfranc almost certainly had his own compilation, a shortened working text of the Pseudo-Isidorian *Decretals*. This appears to have been the parent of nearly a dozen

[7] *The Works of Gilbert Crispin*, ed. A. Abulafia and G. R. Evans (London, 1986).

[8] C. N. L. Brooke, 'Archbishop Lanfranc, the English Bishops and the Council of London of 1075', *Studia Gratiana*, 12 (1967), p.58; and *Councils and Synods*, ed. D. Whitelock, M. Brett and C. N. L. Brooke, vol.1 (871–1204), p.565.

[9] Ibid., pp.613ff., listing items from P. Hinschius, *Decretales Pseudo-Isidorianae* (Leipzig, 1863).

[10] *Councils and Synods*, p.619.

[11] Ibid., p. 674: 'Primum itaque ex auctoritate sanctorum patrum symoniace heresis surreptio in eodem concilio damnata est.'

[12] Ibid., p.675.

[13] F. Ravaisson, *Rapports sur les bibliothèques des départements de l'Ouest* (Paris, 1841), p.375.

English manuscripts of the collection, with copies still in seven cathedral libraries.[14] Lanfranc apparently wanted to be sure of his ground on canon-law questions.

Lanfranc's letters contain a number of references to canon law. These strongly suggest both that he was highly conscious of its importance; and that he was himself sometimes uncertain of the exact character of its rulings – in other words, what the law was. Lanfranc wrote to the Archbishop of Rouen on some suspected error in the matter of ecclesiastical vestments: 'I hear from certain persons that this is being done'; 'But I cannot remember whether that is in accordance with sacred authority'.[15] In Letter 46, Lanfranc notes that Pope Gelasius lists all 'Hilary's' books as catholic texts in his decretal letters. It is probable that he is confusing Pope Hilary with Hilary of Poitiers, but the important point is that he wants to be assured of the authority of the texts he cites and the authors he relies on.[16]

There is evidence in the exasperated letters of Lanfranc and Anselm that the level of episcopal education and performance was not high in eleventh-century England. That cannot have made for alertness to legal implications. In a letter to Herfast, Bishop of Hereford, Lanfranc briskly tells him to give up dicing and other amusements and read the Bible and learn canon law.[17] There is also evidence that Lanfranc was active in seeking to improve the educational level of the English bishops in this area. A pupil of Wulfstan of Worcester called Nicholas was sent to Lanfranc and returned to Worcester as prior.[18]

Canonicity and Legal Vocabulary

The records of the English synods[19] bear the marks of growing sophistication about matters of canon law, but at the same time

[14] Z. N. Brooke, *English Church*, pp.59 and 78; the compilation survives in Trinity College, Cambridge, MS, B.16.44.

[15] *Letters of Lanfranc*, Letter 14, pp.84–5: 'a quibusdam enim id fieri audio'; 'sed utrum id fieri sacris auctoritatibus precipiatur meminisse non valeo'.

[16] Ibid., pp.144–5.

[17] Ibid., Letter 47, pp.150–1: 'decretisque Romanorum pontificum sacrisque canonibus precipue studium impende'.

[18] Z. N. Brooke, *English Church*, p.80.

[19] In *Councils and Synods*, op. cit.

practice was leading theory. Southern thinks *canonica dicta* in Anselm's Letter 77[20] 'means scriptural texts and their authoritative interpreters'. Anselm probably learned what else 'canonical' meant as archbishop. Pope Paschal granted to Anselm the right to grant dispensation from canon law.[21]

'Canonical authority prescribes that a diocese may not remain more than three months without a bishop.'[22] With a similar sense that he is speaking legally, Anselm writes to Samson of Worcester about doing what he ought 'canonically' (and what he is also willing to do).[23] Anselm hears that in Ireland marriages are being dissolved and partners changed, without reasons and against canonical prohibition. He writes to the King about canon law.[24] To the bishops of Ireland, Anselm writes to encourage them to take not only faith but order seriously, and to link canonicity with strictness in their thinking. They are to strive 'manfully in the doctrine of God, with canonical strictness, if anything comes up in their provinces which requires resolution, to ensure that they act according to the will of God'.[25]

Anselm was not spontaneously prompted to an interest in legal questions by his own studies. He was no Ivo of Chartres, and in that respect nor was he a Lanfranc. That means we are, in the later letters, in a period when Anselm's close authorship – as distinct from that of his clerks – cannot be known for certain, but when again and again we meet a sentence or a turn of phrase which does not ring as true Anselm, stylistically or in its content.[26] Nevertheless, we can certainly be sure that he knew and approved

[20] Letter 77, p.68, cf. R. W. Southern, *St Anselm: A Portrait in a Landscape* (Cambridge, 1990), p.72.
[21] Letter 59; cf. R. L. Benson, *The Bishop-Elect: A Study in Mediaeval Ecclesiastical Office* (Princeton, 1968), pp.36–7.
[22] Letter 443, p.390: 'Canonica auctoritas praecepit, ut ecclesia episcopatus ultra tres menses non maneat sine pastore.'
[23] Letter 404, p.349: 'ad faciendum quod de hac re canonice debeo et volo facere'.
[24] Letter 427, p.374, cf. p.435: 'sine ratione palam sine reprehensione contra canonicam prohibitionem commisceri non vereantur'.
[25] Letter 198, p.89: 'viriliter . . . in doctrinam dei, canonica severitate, si quid contra ecclesiasticam doctrinam in provinciis suis intentum fuerit, compescens et secundum dei voluntatem cuncta disponens.'
[26] On this problem of discovering which are the words of a secretary and which the words of the purported author of a letter, cf. Bernard de Clairvaux, *Lettres*, vol.1, ed. M. Duchet-Suchaux and H. Rochais, *Sources chrétiens*, 425 (Paris, 1997), pp.24–6.

the sentiments and instructions which were going out under his name, and it is not wasted effort to look at the legal vocabulary in his letters.

Lex, ius, and *consuetudo* are all familiar usages in Anselm. Anselm writes to Urban II in 1098. He fears that it will appear that he has gone against the law of God, canonical and apostolical authority in adopting voluntary custom.[27] *Iure* is often used by Anselm simply for 'rightly'.[28] But it has its legal connotations, too: *archiepiscopi proprie iuris esset.*[29] Sometimes these are puzzling. *Et quaedam alia ad ius sacerdotum pertinentia*[30] clearly contains a technical term,[31] perhaps drawn from the Council of Carthage of 404. *Lex* for Anselm is pre-eminently *lex dei.*[32] In a letter to Henry, king of England (with a very similar text written to Matilda, queen of England), Anselm puts squarely his insistence that his first duty is to the law of God. He can have made no promise which could override that, whether in his baptism, or in his ordination.[33] No agreement which is against 'the law of Christianity' ought to be followed.[34] Monks have to distinguish between the law of God and their Order's Rule.[35]

For Anselm, custom establishes an 'ought': someone *ought* to act if this is the custom;[36] and 'primas regni sui debet per

---

[27] Letter 206, p.100: 'legem autem dei et canonicas et apostolicas auctoritates voluntariis consuetudinibus obrui videbam. De his omnibus, cum loquebar, nihil efficiebam, et non tam simplex rectitudo quam voluntariae consuetudines obtendebantur.'

[28] For example, Letter 39, p.149, to Lanfranc; Letter 198, p.88, to the bishops of Ireland.

[29] Letter 170, p.51.

[30] Letter 336, p.272.

[31] Cf. Andrew of St Victor, *In Leviticum,* line 856.

[32] Letter 80, p.204; Letter 329, p.262.

[33] Letter 319, p.247 (cf. p.261): 'Neque in baptismo neque in aliqua ordinatione mea promisi me servaturum legem vel consuetudinem patris vestri aut Lanfranci archiepiscopi, sed legem dei et omnium ordinum quod suscepi.'

[34] Ibid., p.424: 'nullum pactum servari debet contra legem Christianitatis'.

[35] Letter 269, p.184: 'Facite ut abbas monasterii Sancti Ebrulfi **revocet** monachos suos quos contra legem dei et ordinem suum in ecclesiam praedic**tam** ingessit, et es eiusdem ecclesiae, quas inde abstulit sacrilegia rapina, iuste restituat'. An interesting usage implying that there are rules for genres, and perhaps indicating that Anselm had a knowledge of the new *ars dictaminis* is: 'Nisi lex epistolae cogeret me'; Letter 101, p.233.

[36] Letter 355, p.297: 'se hoc facere debere per consuetudinem'.

consuetudinem'.[37] The obligation derives in part from the antiquity of such custom.[38] There is *consuetudinem antecessorum*[39] and there is *ex antecessorum consuetudine professi sunt.*[40]

If we turn to the concept of a 'case' (legally speaking), we find a conjoining of 'case' and 'cause' natural to the Latin vocabulary. Anselm consciously lived his life in the *causa dei*, 'God's cause'. That included making decisions on such questions as whether to accept election to Canterbury. He wrote to the monks of Bec on his election to Canterbury, that in a *causa dei* such as this he did not dare to fail to take advice.[41] He continued in the natural presumption that everything he subsequently did as archbishop was in God's cause and all the bishops under him ought to take the same attitude. It was also in the *causa dei* that he wrote to the bishops of Ireland, asking them to send him as their primate cases of a legal sort which they were unable to deal with themselves.[42]

Iudex and *iudicia* are characteristically used by Anselm in connection with God as judge and the *divina iudicia*.

Causa was a term familiar to Anselm both in a wider and in the technically stricter narrow sense of a legal 'case' or dispute 'between' parties. He wrote to Pope Paschal about the dispute between Chartres Cathedral and the local countess.[43] But most importantly of all for his own understanding of the legal framework, he came to see his own dispute with the King as a *causa*. He wrote to Ernulf, prior of Canterbury, to thank him for his help with this *causa*.[44] To Pope Paschal, and the Bishop of Tusculum and Cardinal John, Anselm wrote of the 'cause which is between the King of England and me': *causa [quae est] inter regem Anglorum et me.*[45] In the second of these letters he added a gloss: *immo inter illum et libertatem ecclesiae dei*, 'more: between the King of England and the liberty of the Church of God'. It might be

---

[37] Letter 311, p.236.

[38] Letter 391, p.336: 'vos contra ecclesiasticam consuetudinem in tam grave secundum antiquam consuetudo'.

[39] Ibid.

[40] Letter 472, p.420.

[41] Letter 148, p.5, and Letter 151, p.12.

[42] Letter 198, p.89: 'qua causa quod adiutores me oportuerat habere in causa dei'.

[43] Letter 340, p.278: 'de causa quae est inter Carnotensem ecclesiam et comitissam Carnotensem'.

[44] Letter 331, pp.264, 277, 210, 229.

[45] Letters 338, 388 and 339, pp.276, 31, 277.

a legal case in which he was involved, but it was a bigger issue than that joined between the parties. It was, if we may take the *ecclesia* as then firmly constituting a sector of the public domain, a 'public law' issue.

Anselm's obligations to the King depend, as he understands it, upon the maintenance of right order, the *rectus ordo* which is so strong a feature of the argument of the *Cur Deus Homo*. The King will have none of the pecuniary dues to which he is entitled from the archbishopric until he restores what he has taken from it and canonically reinvests his archbishop in person.[46] Robert of Limminges has become a monk. Anselm grants his wife, during her lifetime, the lands he held of the archbishop. The important point is that she held them of the archbishop not of Anselm. She will continue to hold them if Anselm dies because the grant he has given is binding upon his 'canonical' successor.[47] Here we see Anselm's sense of 'right order' extending to a perception of the distinction between office and person.

There were clarifications of the theology of ministry at the Council of Westminster of 1102. Archdeacons are 'deacons' (the emphasis is that they are not priests). No archdeacon, priest, deacon, or canon may take a wife, or if he takes her, remain with her. Since a subdeacon is not a canon, he may take a wife, but he is bound to live with her chastely once he has taken a vow of chastity. No one is to be ordained subdeacon or above without taking a vow of chastity.[48] A priest in an illicit relationship with a woman may not celebrate the Eucharist and no one should hear his mass if he does so.[49] All these are rulings which go to orderliness and ultimately to 'right order'.

Anselm, as we might expect, is alert to the ground-rules of the theology of ministry and the concomitant branch of 'order'. In a letter to the King of Ireland he describes how bishops are being consecrated without a see to go to and how they are being ordained as though they were priests by a single bishop and not three. Those

[46] Letter 349 to Ernulf, p.288: 'Nullatenus igitur per me aliquid habebit de tota pecunia totius archiepiscopatus, nisi prius me canonice revestierit et ea quae abstulit mihi reddiderit.'

[47] Letter 331 to Ernulf, p.266: 'si hoc tempore factus fuerit monachus, concedo uxori eius, dum vivit, terras quas de me habet; et si quis eas ab alio acceperit nisi ab archiepiscopo Cantuariensi, vel me vel mihi canonice succedente'.

[48] *Councils and Synods*, p.675.

[49] Ibid.

thus instituted are, Anselm instructs, to be deposed from their office together with those who have ordained them: *cum suis ordinatoribus ab episcopatus officio deponi praecipient*. He does not recognize – and probably did not know of – the *chorepiscopus*. He insists that it is for good reason that three bishops are required in the ordination of a bishop. It is a guarantee of their *fides*, *vita* and *sollicitudo*. He also takes it to be fundamental that a bishop must have a *parochia* and a *populum: cui superintendat habeat*.[50] Anselm protests in a letter (*c*.1008) to Ralph, Bishop of Durham, that the bishop-elect of St Andrews cannot be consecrated before the consecration of the archbishop-elect of York.[51]

Jurisdiction and Procedure

There were frequent jurisdictional disagreements *within* the church. Lanfranc's Letter 47 is to Herfast, Bishop of Hereford. Gregory VII instructed Lanfranc to intervene when Herfast attemped to assert his jurisdiction over an exempt abbey. Lanfranc tells Herfast to leave the abbey alone.[52]

But the great issue of the day was the relation of church to state jurisdiction. Anselm went to King William Rufus in 1094 to ask for a council to be called. 'There has not been a general council of bishops in England since you were King', he points out in the words of Eadmer's *History of Recent Events*, 'nor for many years before that'. Meanwhile things have gone from bad to worse. If things are not taken in hand 'the whole land will soon be a Sodom'. He suggests that his pontifical authority and the royal authority should act as one to call a council.[53] The thrust of Anselm's diplomatic letter is to seek to bring both powers on board. It blurs the question of who has jurisdiction.

But the tendency in the administration of justice is the other way, to separate the jurisdictions. The distinguishing feature of

[50] Letter 435, p.383.
[51] Letter 442, p.389: 'hoc nec debet nec potest canonice fieri ab eodem electo archipiscopo, nec ab alio per illum, priusquam ipse fiat archiepiscopus canonica consecratione'.
[52] *Letters of Lanfranc*, pp.150–1: 'quoadus res in nostram audientiam veniat finemque congruum canonica auctoritate nostrique iudicii definitione recipiat'.
[53] Eadmer, *Historia Novorum*, pp.48–9: 'sed conemur una, quaeso, tu regia potestate et ego pontificali auctoritate, quatinus tale quid inde statuatur'.

medieval Church trials is the person before whom they are heard (*coram episcopo, coram archidiacono*).[54] That provides a foundation for a group of rights to be attached to the bishop, and it is noticeable that creeping usurpation of those rights, by lay as well as monastic authorities, was being vigorously checked as it came to be recognized what its implications were.[55] A strong motive for such usurpation was the fine (or share in the fine) it could capture for the usurper.[56]

It seems from pre-Conquest evidence that shire and hundred courts heard both ecclesiastical and secular cases. Bishops were also barons. They could preside over secular courts. Lay and ecclesiastical witnesses might appear side by side.[57] But a bishop already seems to have had a right or duty to deal with certain types of offence both as to judgment and as to penalty. Synods could be courts.[58] A chapter of priests could be a synod. A synod could be held in the chapter house of the cathedral.[59] There is little to suggest that synods were used routinely as courts[60] (as that at Reims was to be in the case of Gilbert of Poitiers in 1148).[61]

William I issued an ordinance to regulate the jurisdiction of bishops in England. He removed ecclesiastical causes from the shire, where the hundred court involved judgment by laymen. Such pleas were now to be reserved to the bishop and the archdeacon.[62] William I's main concern was to ensure that laymen were tried in lay courts and did not seek to slip in under the arm of the church for that purpose.[63] There is ,evidence of separate ecclesiastical

[54] C. Morris, 'William I and the Church Courts', *English Historical Review*, 324 (1967), pp.449–63, at p.450.

[55] Ibid., p.453.

[56] Ibid., p.458.

[57] M. Brett, *The English Church under Henry I* (Oxford, 1975), p.152.

[58] Ibid., p.158.

[59] Ibid., p.155.

[60] Ibid., p.151.

[61] Three kinds of episcopal judgment could be identified: assemblies in which a bishop issued a public judgment; chapters (held in a fixed place) at which as bishop in chapter the bishop delivered a judgment; judgments in synod, which could be given in a variety of locations: ibid., p.134.

[62] Morris, 'William I and Church Courts', p.449.

[63] He issued an ordinance before 1085: 'Propterea mando et regia auctoritate precipio ut nullus episcopus vel archidiaconus de legibus episcopalibus amplius in hundret placita teneant, nec causam que ad regimen animarum pertinet ad iudicium secularium hominum adducant. Sed quicunque secundum episcopales leges de quacumque causa .vel culpa interpellatus fuerit ad locum quem ad hoc

courts after this date.[64] But even by the end of Henry I's reign it is not always clear what law was being administered in ecclesiastical courts, and the crisp identification of courts as courts is not easy. The *Leges Henrici Primi* (*c*.1118), which derive partly from a compilation of Anglo-Saxon laws,[65] still do not distinguish between a tribunal to try lay and a tribunal to try ecclesiastical cases.

The jurisdiction of the church in the immediate post-Conquest period was primarily over moral offences, the relation of sin and crime being in every generation a vexed question.[66] But at the same time it was literally tested 'on the ground' in disputes about property rights and the holding of lands. Most of the cases known to us involve property, for these were the ones recorded in the charter evidence.[67]

Procedure was defined only in a rudimentary way at this date.[68] But there is an emphasis in chapter 5 of the *Leges Henrici* upon the need for due process in all types of case, ecclesiastical and secular (*legaliter et ordine pertractandis*).[69] The compiler of the *Leges Henrici Primi* knew about the *nemo iudex* rule of natural justice. The accusers, the defenders, the witnesses, the judges, must be different persons (*alii; alii*).[70] No judgment is to be given by a judge not approved by the accused:[71] *Iudices sane non debent esse nisi quos impetitue elegerit.*[72] No one is to be judged in his absence.[73] The accused must have a reasonable period in which to prepare his case, and an opportunity to make his defence.[74] There should be no trial until the judge has been agreed.[75] A trial is a formal thing and

episcopus elegerit et nominaverit veniat, ibique de causa vel culpa sua respondeat, et non secundum hundret sed secundum canones et episcopales leges rectum Deo et episcopo suo facia.' *Councils and Synods*, pp.623–4.

[64] Brett, *English Church under Henry I*, p.151.

[65] *Leges Henrici Primi*, ed. L. J. Downer (Oxford, 1972), p.5.

[66] Morris, 'William I and Church Courts', p.451.

[67] Brett, *English Church under Henry I*, p.159.

[68] Morris, 'William I and Church Courts', p.453.

[69] *Leges Henrici Primi*, ch. 5.1, pp.84–5.

[70] Ibid., ch. 5.1, pp.84–5: 'In omni discussione probitatis ydonei nullaque simul exactione permixti'.

[71] Ibid., ch. 5.2.

[72] Ibid., ch. 5.5.

[73] Ibid., ch. 5.3: 'Nec in re dubia vel absente accusato dicta sit sententia'.

[74] Ibid., ch. 5.3: 'et respondendi vel defendendi licentiam legittimam habuerit'.

[75] Ibid., ch. 5.5a: 'Nec prius audiatur vel iudicetur quam ipsi eligantur'.

it has to be properly initiated. There has to be a formal accusation and due process.[76] Christ knew that Judas was a thief, but because Judas was not formally accused he was not found guilty; he was not cast out.[77]

The accused may request adjournments.[78] There must be a right of appeal if there is a procedural flaw or a suspicion of bias.[79] If accusers lay several charges against clerics they shall not be allowed to proceed with the rest if they cannot succeed with the first.[80] A cardinal bishop is not to be condemned except by seventy-two witnesses.[81] For a cardinal priest forty-four witnesses are needed; for a cardinal deacon twenty-six, for a subdeacon seven. No one may judge a pope.[82] Once a secular trial has started it has to finish, but an ecclesiastical case may be halted for good cause.[83]

These are all principles which recur and are developed in the manuals on process stretching forward into the thirteenth century. We have no evidence upon which to credit either Lanfranc or Anselm with their development in England, but these principles of fair procedures must have had their blessing.

So what is new? Certainly there has been a raising of consciousness. England has entered Europe. Lanfranc worked at providing the texts. Anselm, characteristically, kept the deep principles of order always before his eye. For him canon law is a theological study and law and theology should never be separated in the life of the church.

---

[76] Ibid., ch. 5.9a: 'Nec oportet quemquam iudicari vel dampnari priusquam legittimos accusatores habeat . . . locumque defendendi accipiat ad abluanda crimina.'

[77] Ibid., ch. 5.7a.

[78] Ibid., ch. 5.13a.

[79] Ibid., ch. 5.3a: 'Si in testibus et iudicibus et personis satisfactum sit ei, si iudicibus consentiat' [si iudice suspectos habeat] advocet aut contradicat.'

[80] Ibid., ch. 5.10.

[81] Ibid., ch. 5.11.

[82] Ibid., ch. 5.11a.

[83] Ibid., ch. 5.4: 'in ecclesiasticis vero dicta causa recedere licet si necesse fuerit, si iudicem suspectum habuerit vel si se sentiat pregravari'.

2

Lyndwood and the Canon Law: The Papal Plenitudo Potestatis and the College of Cardinals

BRIAN FERME

William Lyndwood remains a key figure in the history of canon law in medieval England, not only because of the number of important positions he held but also because of his celebrated commentary on selected provincial constitutions of the archbishops of Canterbury which he completed in 1433 and which is known as the *Provinciale*.[1] While most of the research devoted to Lyndwood has turned on practical legal questions, one of his earliest and most influential 'students', F. W. Maitland, in the course of proving Lyndwood's reliance on the Roman canon law, necessarily devoted some pages to a consideration of how Lyndwood viewed the papal *plenitudo potestatis*, which was the basis of the legislative and judicial authority that the pope enjoyed.[2]

In reaching his conclusions Maitland had studied the *Provinciale* with an eye to those scattered references to the papal *plenitudo potestatis*. He noticed certain qualifications which affected its exercise: Lyndwood referred to the vexed question of an heretical pope who could be tried by a council as well as pointing to cases in which the specific command of a pope should not be obeyed, as for example the provision of a boy to a benefice *cura animarum*. On

---

[1] For Lyndwood and the *Provinciale*, see B. Ferme, *Canon Law in Late Medieval England: A Study of William Lyndwood's Provinciale with particular reference to Testamentary Law* (Rome, 1996).

[2] For a convenient summary of the questions Maitland addressed, see E. W. Kemp, *An Introduction to Canon Law in the Church of England* (London, 1957), pp.11–32, and R. H. Helmholz, *Roman Canon Law in Reformation England* (Cambridge, 1990), pp.4–12.

the other hand Maitland also noted Lyndwood's claim that no general council could be summoned without the authority of the apostolic see and further noted that Lyndwood had cited without disapproval the opinion of doctors who maintained that the pope was above a general council. Maitland was aware of the limitations of his study but perceptively concluded,

> that an unexampled and irrecoverable opportunity was lost when, in the days between Constance and Basel, the head of the profession wrote a book that was destined to be classical, and hurried past the momentous controversy of the age with a hint, or more than a hint, that the papal was the better opinion. Very recently the archbishop had plucked up courage and had appealed from the pope to a general council. And yet here to all appearance is his learned adviser telling him that any such appeal is vain *quia papa est supra concilium generale*.[3]

Maitland never claimed that his study was comprehensive but given the importance of the *Provinciale* to his overall theory concerning the papal law in medieval England, a reflection of what Lyndwood had to say in his somewhat scattered references to those more general though complex constitutional questions that touched upon the papal authority is relevant.

The debates that centred on the papal *plenitudo potestatis* were the result not only of the crisis caused by the Western Schism but also part of long and detailed reflection on the part of the canonists.[4] An endless number of complex issues required attention: the relationship between the secular and ecclesiastical hierarchies; difficulties between the papal curia and the local episcopate; and tension within the curia itself between the pope and the cardinals. The academic canonists maintained as a general principle that the pope having received sovereign authority from God was himself the source of all inferior authority in the church. None the less, specific problems, as for example the case of an

[3] F. W. Maitland, *Roman Canon Law in the Church of England* (London, 1898), p.15.

[4] For this complex issue, see K. Pennington, *Pope and Bishops: The Papal Monarchy in the Twelfth and Thirteenth Centuries* (Philadelphia, 1984), and *The Prince and the Law, 1200–1600: Sovereignty and Rights in Western Legal Tradition* (Berkeley, 1993); B. Tierney, *Foundations of the Conciliar Theory: The Contribution of the Medieval Canonists from Gratian to the Great Schism* (Cambridge, 1955; repr. 1968); O. Gierke, *Political Theories of the Middle Ages* (Cambridge, 1951).

heretical pope, gave rise to a detailed analysis of the papal *plenitudo potestatis* which seemed to imply that this sovereignty was in particular situations subject to qualification and limitation. There was tension in the writings of many medieval canonists between the theoretical assertions of supreme papal authority and those specific situations which appeared to restrict the exercise of that power.

Naturally we cannot expect to find a systematic study of papal authority or the *plenitudo potestatis* in Lyndwood. His overall aim was considerably different: to expound the legal implications of those various provincial constitutions he had selected and rearranged. On the other hand Lyndwood occasionally reflected on certain issues that involved the papal *plenitudo potestatis,* especially when the constitution or decretal or even word he was glossing raised the question. One such question that was particularly relevant during the Western Schism and continued to be of importance as Lyndwood penned the *Provinciale* was the role of the College of Cardinals and its specific relationship to the pope and the exercise of his *plenitudo potestatis.*

A process of constant centralization, especially since the Gregorian reform of the eleventh century, had notably increased the importance and juridical significance of the College of Cardinals.[5] Yet their legal position with respect to the pope remained open, ill-defined and at times contentious. What function did the cardinals exercise in relationship to a reigning pope in the use of his *plenitudo potestatis?* Were the cardinals for all their dignity and prestige essentially mere agents of the pope? It is true that the canonists conceded great honour and dignity to the sacred college but there was considerable variety of thought when the specific legal questions concerning their relationship to the pope's powers were discussed.

One of the most common ways of analysing this relationship was found in the expression that in matters of major importance or complexity (*in arduis*) the pope acted or disposed of these with the

[5] In general, see G. Alberigo, *Cardinalato e Collegialità: Studi sull'ecclesiologia tra l'XI e il XIV secolo* (Florence, 1969); G. Furst, *Cardinalis: Prolegomena zu einer Rechtsgeschichte des römischen Kardinalskollegiums* (Munich, 1967); S. Kuttner, '*Cardinalis*: The History of a Canonical Concept', *Traditio*, 3 (1945), pp.129–214; J. A. Watt, 'The Constitutional Law of the College of Cardinals: Hostiensis to Johannes Andreae', *Mediaeval Studies*, 33 (1971), pp.127–57.

advice or counsel of the cardinals (*cum consilio fratrum*).[6] Naturally there were cases in which the advice of the cardinals would be offered: in rendering judgments or in making appointments or decisions affecting the *status ecclesiae*. Nevertheless the problem remained of ascertaining in what situations this counsel of the cardinals was or could be considered a restraint upon the papal *plenitudo potestatis*. The cardinals had acquired a right to subscribe to papal decrees and laws were often issued with the formula, *de consilio fratrum nostrorum*, but the precise legal consequences of these passages remained open to discussion.

Lyndwood on the Authority of Cardinals

In a brief but interesting gloss Lyndwood looked at the phrase *de consilio fratrum nostrorum*.[7] While his reflections are clearly not as involved or extensive as those of many of his predecessors, or even a number of his contemporaries, they repay analysis especially given the period in which he lived and composed the *Provinciale*. The schism was still fresh in the minds of many and the debates surrounding the exercise of authority in the church would have been known to Lyndwood. Indeed Maitland reminded us of Chichele's own dispute with Martin V who had been elected by the Council of Constance in 1417.[8]

Lyndwood's gloss can be conveniently divided into two parts. In the first, following Johannes Monachus, Lyndwood refers to the view which held that the pope was bound to consult the cardinals and that this involved a real restriction on his *plenitudo potestatis*. The second part of the gloss, in which he cites Huguccio and Dominicus de Sancto Geminiano, argues instead that the pope is above the cardinals and is not bound to them for his actions.

In the first part of the gloss Lyndwood closely follows Johannes Monachus' argument. He notes, as did Monachus, that the words

---

[6] The phrases *in arduis* and *de consilio fratrum* occur frequently in the *Liber Extra*: X.1.6.54; 1.41.5; 2.13.19; 2.20.28; 3.4.2; 5.31.8; 5.33.23.

[7] *Provinciale*, p.104a. The Oxford 1679 edition has been used.

[8] For a brief discussion of the dispute, see E. F. Jacob, *Archbishop Henry Chichele* (London, 1967), pp.42–60, and R. G. Davies, 'Martin V and the English Episcopate, with Particular Reference to his Campaign for the Repeal of the Statute of Provisors', *English Historical Review*, 92 (1977), pp.309–44.

fratrum nostrorum consilio are *necessitas potius, quam congruentia* basing this on the principle that *ardua negotia* ought to be dealt with *consilio confratrum*. Citing a well-known phrase from the civil law he points out that the pope *licet solutus legibus, tamen secundum leges vivere debet,* and for an explanation of the implications of these ideas we are referred to Monachus' gloss on the *Sext* (VI.5.2.4).[9]

Monachus held quite distinctive views on the authority of the College of Cardinals and there were often sharp differences between his opinions and those of the majority of the canonists.[10] Essentially, he argued that the pope was unable to enact *ardua negotia* without previous consultation with his cardinals. He seems to have wished to establish the principle that pope and cardinals were subject to the same corporation laws as the inferior ecclesiastical colleges, that the pope stood in the same relationship to the cardinals as did any bishop to his cathedral chapter.[11] He came to this conclusion from two papal decisions he claims to have witnessed.

In the first case, Monachus pointed out that Celestine V had appointed many abbots, bishops and other high ecclesiastical dignitaries without having taken the advice of his cardinals. This procedure had been called into question by his successor, Boniface VIII, and Monachus argued that it would be fitting if the pope did not ignore what other popes had ordered to be observed by others. In fact these various collations had been revoked.[12] The second case

---

[9] *Provinciale*, p.104a, a.v. *Fratrum nostrorum Consilio*. A glance at Monachus' gloss a.v. *de consilio fratrum nostrorum* demonstrates Lyndwood's close acquaint-ance with it: 'Quaero an haec sint verba voluntatis, congruentiae, decentiae vel necessitatis . . .'; See Johannes Monachus, *Glossa Aurea super Sexto Decretalium Libro* (Paris, 1535), f.347.

[10] See Tierney, *Foundations*, pp.179–219, and W. Ullmann, *The Origins of the Great Schism* (London, 1972), pp.204–9. Watt, 'Constitutional Law', has argued that Monachus, along with Hostiensis before him and others after him, was not so extreme in his views concerning the powers of the College of Cardinals. He did in fact support the papal *plenitudo potestatis* as against the rights of the cardinals. On the other hand there seems little doubt that Lyndwood saw Monachus as a clear supporter of the cardinals' constitutional rights.

[11] Johannes Monachus, *Glossa Aurea*, f.366: 'Papa sic se habet ad collegium cardinalium, sicut alter episcopus respectu sui collegii . . .'

[12] Ibid.: 'Et scio, quod dictae collationes fuerunt cassatae praesertim, quia coetus cardinalium erat in hac possessione: quod ardua negotia erant de eorum consilio tractanda et terminanda; et in multis iuribus dicitur "de fratrum nostrorum consilio" et licet princeps sit solutus legibus, tamen secundum legis ipsum vivere decet.'

followed a similar pattern. Benedict XI had suspended a number of constitutions which Boniface VIII had promulgated because they had been issued without the advice of the cardinals.[13]

It was generally agreed that the cardinals ought to be consulted in the transaction of business for the Roman Church, but the central issue was whether the pope had such a *plenitudo potestatis* that he could promulgate valid laws *in arduis* without consulting the cardinals. Johannes Monachus tended to the view that he could not. The papal edicts referred to by him had been invalid because they had been promulgated *absque consilio fratrum*. In support he cited the well-known Roman-law principle, *princeps legibus solutus est*, but he emphasized the second part of the citation, *tamen secundum leges ipsum vivere decet*. The principle that a prince ought to obey the laws was underscored by actual cases in which a failure by the pope to do so could be held to have invalidated his enactments. While Monachus was quite prepared to exalt the papal *plenitudo potestatis*, his analysis of its exercise within the Roman See resulted in a real restriction of its use in favour of the cardinals. When discussing Boniface VIII's provision that not even the College of Cardinals could absolve the two condemned Colonna cardinals during a vacancy, Monachus opposed the provision arguing that even the pope's power was subject to specific limitations. While the pope had absolute authority in relation to the rest of the church he was none the less subject in specific ways to the cardinals.[14]

Lyndwood was thus well aware of the view which claimed special prerogatives for the cardinals. On the other hand, the common tradition of the fourteenth century was derived not from Monachus but rather from Guido de Baysio, who considered the very same questions and arrived at distinctly different conclusions. It was in fact this tradition that Lyndwood followed. He commented: 'In hoc contradicunt alii Doctores dicentes, quod Papa

---

[13] Ibid.: 'A benedicto papa xi statuta que dedit marchianis bonifacius pape absque consilio fratrum, quia ardua tangebant, fuerunt suspensa, licet multa iusta fuissent in dictis statutis contenta.'

[14] Ibid.: f.366 ad VI.5.3.1: 'Hic fuit plenitudo potestatis quae subtrahere voluit potestatem aliis competentem . . . item dativa administratio data papae per cardinales non tollit legitimam . . . et papa sic se habet ad collegium cardinalium sicut alter episcopus respectu sui collegii, cum ergo episcopus non possit tollere administrationem legitimam sui capituli, nec papae licebit.'

potest talia expedire sine eis, quia etiam ipse est supra Concilium generale.'[15]

Who were these *alii Doctores*? They were in fact the bulk of the medieval canonists, who while acknowledging as significant the role of the sacred college, nevertheless rejected the view that the pope could not act, except in minor matters, without their approval. The two specifically referred to by Lyndwood were Huguccio and Dominicus de Sancto Geminiano. Lyndwood cites Huguccio's gloss to the *Decretum* (D.4 c.3) arguing that the pope *habet plenitudinem potestatis* and follows by pointing out that the emperor too can do anything that pertains to him without needing the consent of his barons.[16] Huguccio though was somewhat more circumspect than Lyndwood suggests. While pointing out that papal laws ought to be discussed *in consistorio* before promulgation, Huguccio failed to ask the next logical question as to whether laws made without such consultation were thereby invalid.[17]

Lyndwood was well aware of other canonists and the tradition they represented. Thus, Guido de Baysio, with whose writings Lyndwood was well acquainted, argued in his gloss *de consilio fratrum nostrorum*, that this laid down a desirable rule of procedure for the pope which it was proper for him to observe, but it did not bind him *quantum ad necessitatem*.[18] Johannes Andreae, Guido de Baysio's pupil, as well as doubting the truthfulness of Monachus' accounts concerning the revocation of papal decrees, followed a view similar to his master: 'Non compellitur (petere consilia cardinalium), habet enim in se celestis et terreni imperii iura.'[19]

---

[15] *Provinciale*, p.104a.

[16] Ibid.: 'Et hanc partem tenet Hug.4. di.leges. dicens, quod ipse habet plenitudinem potestatis . . . & idem dicit de Imperatore; ut sc. possit quaecunque ad eum spectantia sine consilio suorum Baronum facere.'

[17] See Tierney, *Foundations*, p.81, citing Huguccio's gloss ad D.4 c.3: 'Multa enim consilii consideratione et compatientie maturitate debet discuti et decoqui in consistorio apostolici vel imperatoris lex ante constitutionem.'

[18] Guido de Baysio, *In Sextum Decretalium Commentaria* (Venice, 1577), f.55d, ad VI.1.17.8.

[19] Johannes Andreae, *Novella in Sextum Decretalium* (Lyons, 1550), f.103, a.v. *contingeret* (VI.1.6.17). Andreae expressed incredulity over the stories of Boniface VIII and Benedict XI revoking privileges of their predecessors because they had been made without the consent of the cardinals: 'Hoc ultimum admiror et difficile credo Bonifacium id facisse.'

Dominicus de Sancto Geminiano, glossing VI.5.2.4, argued that Monachus could not be believed because he was a cardinal.[20] It was a point not missed by Lyndwood who cites Sancto Geminiano to question the credence to be given to Monachus' argumentation.[21] This tradition was reflected in the writings of other canonists. Zenzellinus de Cassanis was of the opinion that the pope could dispense with the counsel of the cardinals on the basis of his *plenitudo potestatis*.[22] Albericus de Rosate concluded that the common opinion of the doctors was that the pope had the power to legislate for the universal church even without the cardinals.[23]

It was with the beginning of the Western Schism that the views of Monachus gained support. A near contemporary of Lyndwood, Franciscus Zabarella, wrote an influential tract on the means by which the schism could be healed.[24] In it he argued that the pope alone could not establish a general law affecting the state of the church. He needed the consent of the cardinals, and further he was unable to act in important matters without consulting them.[25] Later in the fifteenth century Andreas de Barbatia could question the views of Dominicus de Sancto Geminiano and defend those of Monachus, citing Zabarella, Panormitanus and Petrus de Anchorano.[26] In many ways, with the onset of the schism, the canonical wheel had turned full circle.

---

[20] Dominicus de Sancto Geminiano, *Lectura super Sexto Libro Decretalium* (Trent, 1522), f.245c: 'Sibi non sit credendum quia cum esset cardinalis conabatur sustinere causam propriam.'

[21] *Provinciale*, p.104a, a.v. *Fratrum nostrorum Consilio*: 'Nec est credendum Johanni Monacho qui erat Cardinalis, & suspectus erat quod voluit sustinere causam propriam, sicut ipsa nota Dominicus de Sancto Geminiano.'

[22] Zenzellinus de Cassanis, *Glossa Ordinaria* to *Extravagantes in Constitutiones Ioannis Papae XXII* (Paris, 1601), gloss ad Clem.1.3.1.

[23] Albericus de Rosate, *Lectura super Codicem* (Lyons, 1518), f.47c: 'Utrum papa sine cardinalibus possit leges sive decretales facere. Laurentius tenet quod non generales . . . communis opinio est in contrarium et etiam de facto servatur.'

[24] Franciscus Zabarella, *Tractatus de Schismate*, in Schardius, *De Jurisdictione Auctoritate et Praeeminentia Imperiali* (Basle, 1566), ff.688–711. The *Tractatus* was part of his commentary on the Decretals as a gloss to I.6.6. See *Super Primo Decretalium Commentario* (Venice, 1602), ff.107c–110b.

[25] Ibid., Schardius, ff. 698–702.

[26] Andreas de Barbatia, *De prestantia Cardinalium, Tractatus Universi Iuris* (Lyons, 1549), f.365a: 'Nec obstat cum dixit dominus Dominicanus non esse credendum Ioan. Monacho cum fuerit cardinalis . . . ad hoc respondeo procedere quando solus Ioan. Monachus hoc dixisset. Sed quando habet multos illustres

Yet it is doubtful whether Lyndwood would have agreed with him. His brief reference to the highly complex problem of the role of the cardinals underlines his cautious approach. He remained very much in the mainstream of canonical thought, following the views of Guido de Baysio rather than those of Johannes Monachus. This is somewhat surprising given the period in which he composed his work, when the whole question of papal power was under close scrutiny and intense academic reflection. He was well aware of this contemporary academic discussion, having read the canonists who dealt with the problem. In addition he would have been aware of Chichele's conflict with Martin V. Nevertheless, the key areas in the debate were left generally untouched. No reference was made to the authority of the cardinals to judge the pope. Their succession to papal authority upon the death of a pope or a vacancy on the papal throne is passed by without comment.

The Purpose of the Provinciale

We should not be too harsh on Lyndwood. He was not involved in the seductions of system building. His contribution continued what had been the essential tasks of canonists in the preceding centuries: not the construction of imposing doctrinal edifices but rather the analysis of concepts, the definition of terms and the investigation of the juridical status of particular institutions and individuals within the church. This should not be too surprising as the fundamental law book of the church, the Corpus Iuris Canonici, was essentially an ordered and systematic collection of particular enactments – for the most part decretals – which were specific responses to particular problems. Academic canonical commentary was necessarily moulded by the structure of the law book it attempted to explain.[27]

One must assume that Lyndwood regarded the issues surrounding the papal *plenitudo potestatis* as either already settled in his mind in favour of the papal *plenitudo potestatis*, or as irrelevant to

doctores contestes qui illud etiam affirmant, tunc ex confirmatione aliorum tollitur illa suspicio.'

[27] For an excellent study on the general characteristics and spirit of the medieval canon law, see R. H. Helmholz, *The Spirit of Classical Canon Law* (Athens, GA, 1996).

his major preoccupation, namely the provision of a practical canonical commentary for the English clergy. This perhaps explains his reluctance to explore too closely the seamier side of ecclesiastical politics, even if this reality did involve critical constitutional legal questions. His concern was with those practical questions that an archdeacon or an *officialis* had to confront in the course of their multifaceted responsibilities. Arguments over the relevant authority of cardinals with respect to the papal *plenitudo potestatis*, while interesting, were in Lyndwood's view distant and far removed from the ever-present realities of failed marriages, property disputes, defamation cases, heresy trials or testamentary issues.

3

The Canons of 1603:
The Contemporary Understanding

RICHARD HELMHOLZ

One of the lasting scholarly contributions made by the Bishop of Chichester has been to question F. W. Maitland's characterization of the medieval canon law. Maitland had described the *Decretales Gregorii IX* (1234) and the canonical collections annexed to it as a book of binding statutes.[1] In a series of lectures delivered at Lichfield Cathedral in 1956, Canon Kemp (as he then was) showed that Maitland's description was anachronistic. Examined in detail, the Decretals read as much like a collection of leading cases as a statute book, and they left considerable room for mitigation through custom, dispensation, and interpretation.[2]

The canons of 1603 stand in an analogous position today. They are commonly understood in anachronistic ways. These 141 canons were adopted by Convocation of the Province of Canterbury in 1603 and subsequently confirmed by letters patent under the Great Seal.[3] They did not receive approval in Parliament, however, as had so much of the Tudor legislation affecting the church. None was sought. Indeed the canons provoked a flurry of hostility in Parliament, although no action ensued.

---

[1] F. W. Maitland, *Roman Canon Law in the Church of England* (London, 1898), p.3.

[2] E. W. Kemp, *Introduction to Canon Law in the Church of England* (London, 1957), pp.16–29.

[3] The text is found in Edward Cardwell, *Synodalia* (Oxford, 1842), vol.1, pp.164–329, including an account of proceedings in Parliament, and is reprinted with facing translation in J. V. Bullard, *Constitutions and Canons Ecclesiastical 1604* (London, 1934). Following recent practice, I have used the date of 1603, the year the Convocation of Canterbury enacted the canons, rather than 1604, when the King agreed to them.

Authority of the 1603 Canons

The starting-point for assessing the authority of these canons has long been an eighteenth-century opinion from the Court of King's Bench, *Middleton v Crofts*.[4] It involved a couple proceeded against in an ecclesiastical court for violating canons 62 and 101–4 by marrying without banns or licence. They procured a writ of prohibition, and the first question was whether the canons bound them at all. The judges held that the canons did not. Parliament had not confirmed them, and canons did not *proprio vigore* bind the laity. The decision went on to qualify this slightly. A canon would bind laymen if it was declarative of 'the ancient usage and law of the church'. In such instances, it would simply be restating or making more definite 'an obligation antecedent to, and not arising from, this body of canons'.[5] The rationale for this exception was that, because the Henrician statutes had expressly preserved existing canon law insofar as it was consistent with the royal prerogative and the laws and customs of England,[6] by implication the medieval canons of the English church had already received parliamentary sanction. From this decision has grown the rule in ecclesiastical law: new canons may bind the clergy and certain ecclesiastical authorities, but they bind no one else.[7]

Despite its widespread acceptance, the King's Bench opinion fits awkwardly with the evidence of how the canons were regarded at the time of their enactment. As Maitland himself noted about the treatment of the medieval law of marriage in *R. v Millis*,[8] English judges may hold an understanding about the law of the church and cause it to prevail in cases coming before them. To some extent, their understanding may even bind their successors. But as a guide

---

[4] 2 Atk. 650 (KB 1736). For modern treatments beginning with this case, see e.g. N. Doe, *The Legal Framework of the Church of England* (Oxford, 1996), p.231; Halsbury's *Laws of England*, vol.14, *Ecclesiastical Law* (4th edn. London, 1975), para.308, pp.142–3.

[5] 2 Atk. at 653.

[6] 25 Hen VIII, c. 19; 27 Hen. VIII, c. 15.

[7] See *Moore's Introduction to English Canon Law*, ed. T. Briden and B. Hanson (3rd edn. London, 1992), p.5; P. Hughes (ed.), *Canon Law and the Church of England* (London, 1955), p.18.

[8] 10 Cl. & Fin. 534 (1843).

to the history, they are not infallible. It may be 'the vanquished cause that will please the historian'.[9] So it is here.

The Contemporary Evidence

The canons themselves give little hint of the doctrine announced in *Middleton v Crofts*. They touched the laity at many points and drew no distinction between 'new' and 'old' law. For example, the canons regulated the qualifications of schoolmasters (c. 77), election of churchwardens (c. 89), probate (c. 93), marriage (c. 100), and defamation (c. 115). They evinced little hesitation about their validity over any class of persons. In the fashion of the times, they subjected to anathema anyone who dared to condemn the authority of this *synodus nationalis* or the canons issuing from it.[10]

Of course, the canons themselves cannot settle the matter. The question is their effect upon the laity, and they cannot be self-validating. However, several other contemporary vantage points are available from which to view the subject. The most informative are the records of the ecclesiastical courts. It was there that the canons were to be enforced. One clearly cannot neglect the common law, however. Perhaps surprisingly, the common law cases stand in general agreement with the evidence from the ecclesiastical forum.

The Common Law

The argument most forcefully pressed in *Middleton* was based on logic, not precedent. The opinion asserted that, because Parliament had repeatedly passed legislation in ecclesiastical matters that bound the laity, it followed that Convocation could not do the same thing. In this view, the existence of such legislation demonstrated the 'constant uniform usage' that laws affecting the laity must first receive parliamentary sanction.[11]

---

[9] F. Pollock and F. W. Maitland, *The History of English Law Before the Time of Edward I* (2nd edn. Cambridge, 1898; repr. 1968), vol.2, p.372.

[10] Cardwell, *Synodalia*, cc. 139–41.

[11] 2 Atk. at 657.

Contemporary understanding of the relation between Parliament and Convocation was, however, rather different from what this argument assumed. Canons were by-laws passed by Convocation to supplement the general law of the church. No one considered them 'co-extensive' with Acts of Parliament, as the opinion repeatedly asserted they must have been if they had been thought capable of binding the laity. Just as the medieval provincial canons could not contradict the general law of the church, so the 1603 canons could not contradict the law enacted by Parliament. But that did not mean that Convocation had no independent power at all, before or after the Reformation, and it had little relevance to the question of distinguishing between the authority of canons over the laity and the clergy.

Focusing attention on pre-1640 decisions of the common law courts makes it hard to find support for the principal resolutions in *Middleton*. Indeed, in so far as they are in point, the cases only raise obstacles to accepting the opinion as history. For instance, the opinion placed a great deal of weight on two fifteenth-century Yearbook cases. In one of them Newton J. had stated that Convocation, 'cannot do anything that binds the temporality'.[12] However, despite its apparent relevance, the fit between this statement and the facts in *Middleton* was awkward. The Yearbook cases involved grants of a tenth by Convocation to the King. In refusing to pay his assigned portion, a cleric had proffered a charter of exemption from the King, and his refusal was upheld. The case therefore did not involve the laity at all. Moreover, as it stated, the tenth, once granted, was regarded as a temporal obligation.[13] All that the two cases held was that in such temporal matters, the church had no authority to overthrow a grant by the King. This was a traditional rule in English law. The pope himself had no authority to legislate in temporal matters. These cases happened to involve Convocation, but in fact they merely drew a

---

[12] *Prior of Leeds Case* (KB 1441), YB Mich. 20 Hen. VI, pl. 25: 'ils ne poient faire ascun chose qui lier la temporalte'.

[13] YB Mich. 20 Hen. VI, pl. 25: 'uncore quand disme est grante, ceo est chose temporel en le Roy', *per* Fray; 'le Roy peut discharger le Prior de tiel chose qui est temporelle par ses letters', *per* Hody CJ. The determinative question seems to have been whether the prior, present in Convocation in the eyes of the law, had thereby renounced use of the royal grant.

conclusion from the traditional common law rule that a division existed between authority in temporal and spiritual spheres.

The other cases cited in support of its resolution by *Middleton* all either rested upon this same distinction or upon the question of whether or not a canon could overturn a custom established by prescription.[14] The second of these was a contentious matter, as much so in the spiritual forum as it was in the temporal. However, it revolved around an old question in the *ius commune*: the extent to which a custom could lawfully derogate from a legislative enactment. The answer to it determined the rights of the clergy as fully as it did those of the laity. The judges did not come to grips with this point. Perhaps they did not see it.

They did, however, have to face several common law cases that appeared to support the argument that the effect of the canons was not limited to the clergy.[15] A case cited from Rolle's *Abridgement*, for example, upheld the validity of canon 93, setting a minimum value of £5 to constitute *bona notabilia* for jurisdictional purposes in estate administration. The judges treated this as merely restating a rule from the ancient canons,[16] even though the *Abridgement* itself states, '[I]t seems that this canon has changed the law, which before was otherwise'.[17] Another was a case in Chancery decided three years after the canons were issued, in which Coke, Popham and Fleming JJ also participated. It resolved, '[T]he canons of the Church made by Convocation and the King without Parliament will bind in all ecclesiastical matters, just as an Act of Parliament'.[18] *Middleton* set this authority aside, because it was said to be 'a very extraordinary case' and because, 'it is not expressly said

[14] *Gaudye v Newman* (CP 1610) 2 Brownl. & Golds. 38; Of Convocations, 12 Co. Rep. 72 (1610); *Jermyn's Case* (KB 1623), Cro. Jac. 670; *Orme v Pemberton* (KB 1640), Cro. Car. 589.

[15] The closest case factually arose later: *Hill v Good* (CP 1673), Vaughan 302. It involved an attempt to prosecute a man and woman for contracting an incestuous marriage. Invoking canon 99, the report states, at 327, that just as an Act of Parliament may make a union incestuous, 'By the same reason, if by a lawful canon a marriage be declared to be against God's law, we must admit it to be so: for a lawful canon is the law of the kingdom, as well as an Act of Parliament'. *Middleton v Crofts*, 2 Atk. at 667, concluded that this precedent 'proves nothing in the present case, because it is silent, and does not determine what is necessary to make a lawful canon'.

[16] 2 Atk. at 659. The opinion seems finally to concede the point.

[17] Rolle's *Abridgement*, tit. executor (I)(5).

[18] *Bird v Smith* (Chanc. 1606), Moore 781, at 783.

they [the canons] can bind the laity'.[19] A more natural reading would be that the case drew no distinction between a canon's effect on the laity and the clergy because, in matters properly within ecclesiastical cognizance, the distinction did not then exist.

Examining contemporary common law prohibition cases only deepens one's doubts. These centuries witnessed the creation of new grounds for restraining the exercise of ecclesiastical jurisdiction.[20] Where an ecclesiastical court presumed to interpret a statute, determine the validity of a custom, or indirectly affect the course of the common law, a writ of prohibition might issue to prevent it from acting. Some cases went so far as to suggest that the ecclesiastical courts could not apply the two-witness rule or make use of the oath *ex officio*. However, in this developing law, one searches in vain for cases prohibiting ecclesiastical proceedings simply because a canon had been enforced against a layman. The idea does not seem to have been raised.

Richard Hooker

In seeking to understand contemporary opinion about the canons, the opinions of men who were not lawyers should not be excluded. They can provide a fuller picture. If one seeks a representative voice of the church, Richard Hooker comes about as close as one could hope. Although scholars disagree about where to place Hooker in the history of Western thought, there is little dispute that he was a spokesman for the Elizabethan church. Hooker also discussed (and knew something about) the laws of the church,[21] although he had no formal legal training and was certainly not a professional civilian. He wrote to defend the church from those he considered its enemies and to persuade them if he could. That required dealing with the church's law.

---

[19] 2 Atk. at 667.

[20] See C. Gray, *The Writ of Prohibition: Jurisdiction in Early Modern English Law*, 2 vols. (New York, 1994).

[21] See e.g. his 'Autograph Notes', in *The Folger Library Edition of the Works of Richard Hooker* (gen. ed., W. Speed Hill), 6 vols. (1977–93) [hereafter cited as Folger Edition], vol.3, ed. P. Stanwood (Cambridge, MA, and London, 1981), pp.462–538. These notes reveal some command of the *ius commune*, e.g. at 470, appear citations of Guido de Baysio, Hostiensis, Johannes Andreae, and Innocent IV.

Hooker obviously could not have commented on the authority of the 1603 canons. He died just before their enactment. However, his *Of the Lawes of Ecclesiastical Polity* had much to say about ecclesiastical law in general and the place of canons in particular. Hooker was in no doubt that the church must be governed by law. The dangers inherent in a regime of private judgment were manifest.[22] That the church itself had the power to ordain laws for its members he thought equally clear. Such regulation had been within the power of the church since the Council of Jerusalem, and so it continued to his day.[23]

Moreover, within limits set by Scripture and the law of nature, the laws of the church could be changed as time and circumstance required. This argument was directed against those who maintained that only laws contained in the Gospels bound the Christian.[24] Hooker maintained that the church had no less power 'to ordeine that which never was then to ratifie what hath bene before'.[25] It would be 'absurd to imagine the Church itselfe . . . abridged of this libertie', or to suppose that 'noe law, constitution, or canon, can be further made'.[26] It was also certain that this included power to 'exact obedience at the hands of hir own children'.[27] Citing Gratian's *Decretum*,[28] Hooker even ventured the opinion that canons were made 'by instinct of the Holy Ghost'.[29]

Granting this authority to the church's legislation did not mean that its power to bind either clergy or laity was absolute. Here Hooker stood within medieval traditions. Applying a statute was not simply a matter of checking the appropriate 'rule of recognition' and then enforcing the statute's terms. Legislation was to be measured against natural and divine law.[30] It must not contradict the Scriptures, and it must conform to the law of nature that God

[22] E.g., *Of the Lawes of Ecclesiastical Polity*, V.20.9–10 [hereafter *Lawes*], in Folger Edition, giving citations by book, chapter and section.

[23] *Lawes*, III.10.2, citing the *Decretum*, C. 1 q. 1 c. 41.

[24] *Lawes*, III.9.3.

[25] Ibid., V.8.1.

[26] Ibid., VI.1.4–2.2. See also VII.14.3: the church 'hath the same Authority still, and may abrogate old Laws, or make new, as need shall require'.

[27] Ibid., V.8.4.

[28] C. 25 q. 1 c. 5.

[29] *Lawes*, III.8.18.

[30] Ibid., III.9.2: '[L]awes humane must be made according to the generall lawes of nature, and without contradiction unto any positive law in scripture'.

has implanted in our hearts. Hooker invoked the traditional adage that law received its strength from the assent of those who were governed by it.[31] He recognized the claims of conscience against laws that worked iniquity in particular cases, as had medieval jurists, and he was at pains to adduce the traditional limitations to those claims.[32]

Moreover, in applying statutes it was always important that judges consider the purpose for which a particular law had been adopted – what Hooker called the 'foreconceaved ende for which it worketh'.[33] This consideration might show that the reason for it had passed. If so, the rule of desuetude meant that the statute applied no longer.[34] Or it might be that the statute itself had not been meant to apply where there was an established custom to the contrary.[35] One could only tell by analysis. The law of the medieval church was simply not a regime of 'binding statute law' in the sense we understand the phrase today, and it was about this law that Hooker wrote.

Attachment to medieval traditions did not keep Hooker from defending the force of parliamentary statutes and royal supremacy in ecclesiastical matters. With citation of Scripture, Christian history, Roman law, and the canon law itself,[36] he sought to prove that the 'whole body of this Realme' had the authority to establish laws governing the church.[37] This was difficult to reconcile with the medieval canon law, which excluded the laity from the exercise of authority within the church wherever it could, and in his refusal to exclude the laity from decision-making within the church, Hooker spoke for the traditions of Anglicanism. But this does not make him a proponent of the later reading of the effect of English canons. Indeed, it does not seem to have occurred to him that, by endorsing the power of the English Parliament to legislate for the English church, he was thereby excluding the making of any canons whose reach extended beyond the clergy. In his view, the

---

[31] Ibid., VIII.6.11: '[I]t is the generall consent of all that giveth them the forme and vigor of lawes'.
[32] Ibid., VIII.6.9.
[33] Ibid., I.2.1.
[34] Ibid., III.10.2, again citing the *Decretum*.
[35] *Lawes*, II.5.7.
[36] See e.g. ibid., VIII.7.5.
[37] Ibid., VII.6.7; VIII.1.2; VIII.6.11.

canons of 1603 should be enforced in much the same way their medieval antecedents had been.

The Ecclesiastical Courts

The most direct evidence about the extent to which the 1603 canons were enforced comes from the archives of the ecclesiastical courts. A good deal has survived. Act books and other records of the courts show that the canons were regularly applied in cases involving the laity, although questions about their effectiveness were raised from the moment of their enactment. Perhaps evidence of what actually happened in the spiritual forum does not count in the course of the development of English common law. It counted then. And it must also count for the historian.

Enforcement of the 1603 canons built upon medieval experience. English lawyers, ecclesiastical as well as secular, recognized no fundamental difference between the authority of most precedents from before and after the break with Rome, except of course with respect to the rights of the papacy.[38] They accorded a large role to canons adopted in provincial councils and synods. The law of testamentary succession, for example, was largely dependent upon the fourteenth-century constitutions of Archbishop Stratford.[39] The whole law of defamation took its origins from a provincial constitution of 1222.[40] These constitutions were not, of course, regarded as contrary to the general canon law. They simply supplemented it. However, in both theory and practice, they were applied to the laity.

In much the same fashion as the medieval constitutions had been, the canons of 1603 were put into effect by the spiritual

[38] E.g. 'Of Convocations', 12 Co. Rep. 72 (1610), maintaining that the statute, 25 Hen VIII, c. 19, 'was but an affirmance of what was before the said statute'.

[39] William Lyndwood, *Provinciale (seu Constitutiones Angliae)* (Oxford, 1679), 171. The constitutions were the common source of ecclesiastical causes brought to enforce the last wills of decedents; e.g. BL, MS. Reg. 11.A.XI, ff. 41v–42 (a fourteenth-century ecclesiastical court formulary).

[40] *Councils and Synods with other Documents Relating to the English Church,* ed. F. M. Powicke and C. R. Cheney (Oxford, 1964), pt.1, p.107. The canon was commonly recorded as the source of law on this subject; e.g. *Davy c. Trendall* (Norwich, 1510), Norfolk RO, Norwich, ACT 1, s.d. 7 June; the defendant was alleged by his slander to have incurred, 'sentenciam in constitutione provinciali que sic incipit Ex auctoritate dei patris omnipotentis . . .'

courts. They were applied *proprio vigore* to both laity and clergy. Nor did practice recognize a requirement that they impose 'an obligation antecedent to, and not arising from this body of canons'. For example, canon 100 provided that no child under the age of twenty-one should contract marriage without the consent of their parents or guardians. No such prohibition existed in the medieval law, but the canon was regularly put into execution in the ecclesiastical courts.[41] Canon 115 granted a partial immunity from being sued for defamation to churchwardens who made presentments during visitations. This was a reform – a sensible one in light of the increasing responsibilities being placed upon churchwardens – and it was put into effect.[42] So was canon 91, which regulated the choice of the parish clerk.[43] This particular canon often came into conflict with long-established parochial customs, and it was open to challenge on that account. But this was a quite different objection under the ecclesiastical law of the time than asserting that it had no effect *proprio vigore* upon the laity.

However regular their enforcement, the new canons were also controversial from the start. We can observe the controversies. The years between 1603 and 1640 witnessed the collection of legal material by civilians for their own use, mostly reports of cases in the ecclesiastical courts and commentary about them. They allow us to see, as formal records do not, the arguments made about the force of the canons. They show clearly that the canons were the

---

[41] E.g. *Ex officio c. Bradford* (Hereford 1638), Hereford RO, Act book O/98, s.d. 10 November: 'detected maried without consent of parentes'. Another example: *Ex officio c. John Barber* (Canterbury 1618), Cathedral Archives, Canterbury, X.9.14, f.9, brought against the young man who had married an underage girl without her mother's consent.

[42] See Borthwick Institute, Prec.Bk.11, f.10v (c.1610): 'No judge will admit an action against the churchwarden, because it is to be presumed he doth it not upon malice'. See also manuscript copy of Francis Clerke's *Praxis in curiis ecclesiasticis*, Catholic University of America, Washington, DC, Library Special Collections, MS. 180, f.238, *marginalia*: 'Vide canon 115 qui repugnat et tollit huiusmodi actionem quoad gardianos'.

[43] *Hobson v Sanderson* (York 1624), Borthwick Institute, HC.CP.1624/10, in which the plaintiff alleged that the choice 'belongeth unto him by the canons and ecclesiastical constitutions of the Church of England'. Another example: *Ex officio c. Bird* (Chichester 1613), West Sussex RO, Ep I/17/15, s.d. 26 June, a cause brought to enforce the canon that churchwardens were to be chosen jointly by the incumbent and the parishioners.

subject of dispute, but the dispute was framed in terms of traditional rules, not those of *Middleton v Crofts*.

Two principal matters of contention arose. The first was the relationship between the canons and statutes. It was generally agreed that Acts of Parliament prevailed wherever there was incompatibility between them and the canons. The point was succinctly made in an early seventeenth-century case involving a collision between canon 122 and a statute of 1545: where such direct opposition existed, the canon is 'to litle purpose against a statute of the realme'.[44]

The more contentious question arose indirectly in connection with changes in the law of the church. The Henrician statutes preserved existing canon law insofar as it was not repugnant to the royal prerogative or to the law and customs of the realm. An argument could be made, therefore, that these statutes had in effect 'frozen' the law in the state it was in 1535. What the statutes preserved took on the added force of English statute law, and a statute prevailed over a canon to the contrary. If this interpretation was correct, few parts of the medieval canon law could be changed except by Parliament.

However, the *communis opinio* among the civilians rejected it. The nature of the argument is illustrated by a case involving the power of the ecclesiastical courts to excommunicate, now found in an early seventeenth-century proctor's notebook in the British Library.[45] Most spiritual courts were presided over by men not in holy orders. When required to issue a sentence of excommunication, they called upon a clergyman to read the formal sentence. Was this procedure lawful? The question divided this into two halves. The first – which today seems the most difficult – was not in real doubt. The exercise of spiritual jurisdiction by laymen was authorized by a statute.[46] The other half was the more difficult. The canon law formally restricted the power to excommunicate to bishops.[47] The question was thus whether clerics who were not bishops could lawfully excommunicate, as they did in English practice. The proctor correctly noted that 'the laws do not permit

[44] Borthwick Institute, York, Prec.Bk.11, f.40v, a case involving authority to deprive an incumbent of his benefice.
[45] BL Add. Ms. 6254, f.36.
[46] 37 Hen. VIII, c. 17.
[47] C. 16 q. 2 c. 1; the rule was subject to a number of exceptions.

that the power of excommunicating can go to a simple priest'.[48] The notebook's entry nevertheless upheld the validity of this English usage, and it cited a provincial canon as authorization for it.[49] However, it also cited the force of local custom and the medieval commentaries by Panormitanus and Lyndwood in support.[50]

The approach of this case was in line with the *communis opinio* among the English civilians. They took the view that the Henrician statutes did not prevent changes in the law by Convocation.[51] The statutes were general in their wording, and they did not forbid alterations in the law. As such, they left existing principles of law intact, including the power to amend the church's law when necessary. Common usage in the courts confirmed the strength of that position. By the same token, this was a real argument, and when English canons changed the canon law, the civilians liked to have as many strings to their bow as they could.

The second point of contention relating to the canons involved their relationship to established local customs. Disputes about this arose frequently. The position most frequently taken among the civilians is illustrated by an extract from a manuscript of ecclesiastical causes now at York's Borthwick Institute:[52]

The canons of the Convocation house, by reason they are not confirmed by act of Parliament, doe take no place but when there is no lawe or custome to the contrary. Exempli gratia: The canon 89 prescribe an order for choyce of churchwardens by the minister and the parishioners, yett in some parishes they have use for time out of minde that the ould churchwarden shall appoint one. This custome must prevayle against the canon. But such points in the canons as are otherwise by statute prescribed or by iniunction observed for longe

---

[48] BL Add. MS. 6254, f.36: 'Hoc vero jura non concedunt, ut simplici sacerdoti potestas sit excommunicandi.'

[49] Cardwell, *Synodalia*, vol.1, p.155.

[50] Panormitanus, *Commentaria* ad X 1.31.2, no. 8, after stating the difficulty and citing contrary opinion, adopts the view favouring the practice. The text from Lyndwood (*Provinciale*, 196 s.v. *censuris*) also supports it.

[51] E.g. 'Certaine adjudged cases in the civill lawe' (c.1620), Oxford, Bodl. MS. Eng.misc.f.473, p.4: '*Quaere* here whether any part of the common law used in England may be repealed by an act of the convocation treated and assented unto by the kinges assent. I think yea.'

[52] Prec.Bk.11, f.22. See also R. D. H. Bursell, 'What is the Place of Custom in English Canon Law?', *Ecclesiastical Law Journal*, 1 (4) (1989), pp.12–26.

time, must be kept precisely, as such orders as are in the Communion booke, which is confirmed by act of Parliament.

In other words, this civilian took the view that this canon did not prevail against a valid local custom to the contrary. This position left some room for manœuvre, as treatment of customs in the *ius commune* always had. It was not always easy to meet the standards for proving a custom, and customs had to survive an inquiry into their reasonability. However, established local customs might set real limits to Convocation's ability to amend the ecclesiastical law. Only when canons enacted something genuinely new did they not confront this obstacle. This result, it should be noted, is very like the exact opposite of the holding in *Middleton v Crofts*. What Convocation could *not* easily do was to enact a canon affecting 'an obligation antecedent to, and not arising from, this body of canons'. However, if no valid custom existed, the path was opened to legislation.

Conclusion

The 1603 canons were controversial. Under some circumstances they were not 'binding statute law'. They might be invalid because of a contrary custom, and they might fail if they came into conflict with a statute. In the course of time, they might fail because of desuetude. But no contemporary distinction was drawn between their effect on the clergy and on the laity. The question was to determine the circumstances in which they bound anyone at all, and this was a question largely carried over from the medieval *ius commune*.

Does this history make any difference for the present? It may. That is not for me to say. I am a foreigner, and what I know about the law of the church comes mostly from the law of the Middle Ages. I do think, however, that to the extent what I have read about the current movement 'towards autonomy' from parliamentary control in the Church of England goes forward,[53] the movement will actually be a return to something like the situation that existed in the years following enactment of the 1603 canons.

[53] See M. Hill, *Ecclesiastical Law* (London, 1995), p.19.

4

The Strange Afterlife of the Reformatio Legum Ecclesiasticarum

GERALD BRAY

On 5 November 1551 a royal commission was appointed in the name of King Edward VI to carry out a complete reform of the English canon law.[1] This Commission had been a long time coming, having first been mooted by Edward Fox, the royal almoner, in his address to the Convocation of Canterbury on 10 May 1532, and then being mentioned in several statutes during Henry VIII's reign,[2] without however being constituted. The need for such a commission grew initially out of Henry's difficulties in obtaining an annulment of his marriage to Katharine of Aragon, a problem which was a canon-law dispute, but after the break with Rome the issue took on a much wider dimension as it became clear that the Church of England could not continue to use a canon law which presupposed the papacy and the Roman supremacy which went with it. In principle, the commission was meant to consist of thirty-two experts, drawn in equal measure from the clergy and the laity, who in the 1551 commission were further subdivided into upper and lower clergy, on the one hand, and civil and common lawyers on the other. The actual letter of appointment mentioned only eight names, drawn equally from each of these four categories, and although lists of the thirty-two are extant, it is not known how many of them played any real part in the commission's deliberations. What is certain is that Archbishop Cranmer, who probably chaired the committee, revised a draft document, which

---

[1] In accordance with 3–4 Edward VI, c. 11 (1549).
[2] 25 Henry VIII, c. 19 (1533); 27 Henry VIII, cc. 15 and 20 (1535–6); 35 Henry VIII, c. 16 (1543–4).

was ready sometime in 1552, and which has survived among the Harleian manuscripts at the British Library.[3] It is also certain that Peter Martyr Vermigli had a hand in this revision, as did Dr Walter Haddon, Master of Trinity Hall, Cambridge, although he was not a member of the commission. Beyond that, we can only speculate.

On 10 April 1553 Cranmer presented the text to the House of Lords, where it was criticized and rejected by John Dudley, Duke of Northumberland and effective head of the government. Cranmer and Northumberland were never close, and the latter seems to have objected in principle to the kind of church discipline which adoption of the document would have imposed on the laity as well as on the clergy. Many people, however, felt that in due course the king would have approved it if he had lived to attain his majority, and that its failure to pass in 1553 was therefore due to a political accident rather than to any deep difference of policy between the spiritual and the temporal authorities. As it was, Edward VI died on 6 July 1553 and both Cranmer and Northumberland were removed from power as soon as Mary I gained control. The reformed canon law disappeared, although it was resurrected under Elizabeth I and put forward as a possible element in her settlement of religion. The precise turn of events is hidden from our eyes, though there was apparently a suggestion in 1563 that convocation should revise the canons along the same lines as the Articles of Religion and the Book of Common Prayer. What happened next is obscure, but in 1571 the text was finally published by John Foxe and offered to the House of Commons by Thomas Norton, son-in-law of the late Archbishop Cranmer and owner of the manuscript which is now in the British Library.[4]

The *Reformatio Legum Ecclesiasticarum*,[5] as Foxe called his edition, was not accepted by Parliament, and no more was heard of it. Instead, convocation drafted new canons, which made some use of the *Reformatio*, to which the Queen gave her approval, though they were never formally ratified.[6] Foxe's text disappeared once

---

[3] Harleian MS 426.

[4] Foxe used this MS in preparing his edition, but the printed text is based primarily on another, fuller copy which was then in the possession of Archbishop Parker. It is now missing.

[5] Abbreviated in the notes as *RLE*.

[6] For these canons and the contribution of the *Reformatio* to them, see G. L. Bray, *The Anglican Canons 1529–1947* (Woodbridge, 1998), pp.172–209.

more, although it was republished (with corrections) in 1640 and again in 1641,[7] when the canon law was once more a matter of dispute. The *Reformatio* might reasonably be said to represent 'Puritan conformity', i.e. a strict church discipline within the traditional establishment, and in the early 1640s adoption of it must have seemed to some to offer a reasonable solution to the political and religious crisis of the time. Once again, nothing happened and the *Reformatio* disappeared, this time for good. The restored church of 1660 was in no mood to consider it as a possible way forward, nor did it resurface in the more accommodating atmosphere of 1689, when a serious attempt was made to adapt the Church of England in a way which would comprehend as many Nonconformists as possible. Given that the *Reformatio* had little of the latitudinarian spirit which dominated those attempts at reconciliation, we should not be surprised at this – its strict discipline could never have been adapted to the needs of religious comprehensiveness as this was understood in the late seventeenth century, and its survival owed much to the efforts of someone who was of quite a different ecclesiastical stamp.

Gibson's Codex

Edmund Gibson (1669–1748), Bishop of Lincoln from 1716 and of London from 1723, was the author of the famous *Codex Iuris Ecclesiastici Anglicani* (1713), which rapidly established itself as the *vademecum* of ecclesiastical lawyers.[8] While he was vicar of Lambeth (1704–10), Gibson collected all the material which made up the ecclesiastical law of England, and arranged it in a systematic order. He then added his own commentary, which became the standard interpretation of the texts in which he drew on the *Corpus Iuris Canonici*, the *Corpus Iuris Civilis*, the

---

[7] The 1640–1 editions do not differ in any substantial way from that of 1571, though they correct a number of errors and supposed errors which had crept into the earlier text. In the eighteenth century, Gibson used Foxe's edition, but most early nineteenth-century references are taken from the later text. Both were effectively superseded by Edward Cardwell's critical edition in 1850.

[8] For a recent assessment of Gibson, see J. H. Baker, 'Famous English Canon Lawyers VIII: Edmund Gibson and David Wilkins', *Ecclesiastical Law Journal*, 17 (1995), pp.371–8, reproduced and revised in J. H. Baker, *Monuments of Endlesse Labours: English Canonists and their Work, 1300–1900* (London, 1998), p.95.

Provinciale of William Lyndwood, and the *Reformatio Legum Ecclesiasticarum*. His motive for including the last of these is stated quite explicitly in the preface:

> The citations of ancient and modern councils and synods which have been held at home and abroad (as they are annexed here by way of commentary to our present laws) are designed to show, on one hand, that though many of the laws are modern, the constitution is ancient; and on the other hand to facilitate the improvement of this constitution by suggesting such useful rules of order and discipline as have been established abroad or attempted at home. With which last view it is that many of the passages out of the body of ecclesiastical laws entitled *Reformatio legum etc.* are grafted into this commentary as candidates for a place in our constitution in case the convocation shall think them deserving, or at least as not unworthy the consideration of that learned and venerable assembly.[9]

Gibson's hope was not to be realized, because only four years after his *Codex* appeared, business transactions in convocation were suspended, not to be resumed on a regular basis until 1852. But that was not to make much difference, because Gibson quoted from the *Reformatio* in such a way as to grant it surrogate authority, regardless of what any legislative body might have said about it.

Gibson was well aware of the history of the text, and included a full account of it in the *Codex*. But although he knew that the *Reformatio* had no official status, the way in which he handled it tells a rather different story. For instance, he not infrequently quoted it as a handy summary of earlier, more complex legislation, thereby granting it practical authority as a work of reference without pronouncing on its legal status. A good example of his technique can be found in what he has to say about the royal supremacy, where he quotes *Reformatio* 37.2[10] as a useful statement of how that was viewed in the time of King Edward VI. He does the same with many other matters, including the absolution of those who have laid violent hands on a clergyman,[11] the

---

[9] E. Gibson, *Codex Iuris Ecclesiastici Anglicani* (London, 1713), p.xiv.

[10] All citations from the *Reformatio* are according to the chapter divisions adopted for the author's forthcoming edition. A list of these can be found in Bray, *Anglican Canons*, pp.888–9.

[11] Gibson, *Codex*, I.4 (10–11), quoting *RLE* 48.1–2.

alienation of ecclesiastical property,[12] simony,[13] the office of rural deans,[14] the procedure for appeals,[15] the commutation of penance[16] and excommunication.[17] In each of these instances Gibson is claiming only that the *Reformatio* is summarizing and repeating earlier legislation, but the fact that he quotes it rather than the legally correct sources shows that he accepted it as authoritative when it was summarizing earlier legislation.

But once the *Reformatio*'s usefulness in this respect was established, it was but a short step to regarding it as proof of sixteenth-century practice, whether there was any evidence to support this or not. Gibson was not averse to doing this, particularly when its rules looked eminently desirable. A good example of this can be found in what he had to say about the resignation of a clergyman from his benefice. Traditionally, this could be done by proxy, but Gibson did not think that that was a good idea, and neither did the *Reformatio*, which insisted than a man resign his benefice in person. So Gibson simply overrode Lyndwood's testimony, as well as the evidence of traditional writs (both of which he mentioned), and stated categorically that resignation must be made in person, citing the *Reformatio* as his only source for this.[18] He dealt in a similar way with the penalties to be inflicted on those who ignore orders of suspension, even going so far as to pronounce the laity excommunicate on the sole basis of the *Reformatio*'s authority.[19] He did the same again when he claimed that the church has the right to proceed in a spiritual way against criminals, after sentence in the temporal courts,[20] and also when he rejected leniency in the commutation of penance.[21] The fact that these were extremely sensitive matters, particularly where the laity were involved, makes his audacity all the more remarkable.

[12] Ibid., XXX.1 (688), quoting *RLE* 16.1.
[13] Ibid., XXXIV.4 (840–1), quoting *RLE* 11.24.
[14] Ibid., XLII.8 (1011–12), quoting *RLE* 20.5.
[15] Ibid., XLV.6 (1080), quoting *RLE* 54.26.
[16] Ibid., XLVI.3 (1092), quoting *RLE* 28.11.
[17] Ibid., XLVI.4 (1095), quoting *RLE* 32.3–4.
[18] Ibid., XXXIV.11 (869), quoting *RLE* 12.5.
[19] Ibid., XLVI.3 (1093), alluding to *RLE* 29.5.
[20] Ibid., XLV.5 (1078), quoting *RLE* 32.16.
[21] Ibid., XLVI.4 (1095), quoting *RLE* 32.4.

It is true that Gibson recognized that the *Reformatio* has a pre-scriptive side which was never realized in practice, and he occasionally mentioned this, as when he suggested that coadjutors should be appointed to assist incapacitated bishops,[22] that bishops should attend the examination of future incumbents in person,[23] that parental consent for underage marriages should be com-pulsory[24] and that Sunday schools should be formed for instructing the young.[25] On these and other matters it was impossible to pretend that things had once been different, nor could Gibson simply lay down the law.[26] Here more than anywhere, the stated intention of his preface comes to the fore. But there is one instance in which Gibson mentions an actual court case in which the decision appears to derive from rules laid down in the *Reformatio*. It concerned the question of whether illegitimate relations counted in the table of kindred and affinity, and Gibson commented that there were two rules in the *Reformatio Legum* which help us to understand what they are. He then went on to quote a case[27] in which a man was charged for marrying his sister's bastard daughter, and it appears that the principles of the *Reformatio* were actually applied.[28]

The Reformatio Rediviva

Of course, Gibson's attempt to rescue the *Reformatio Legum* from oblivion did not change the law, and the practice of the ecclesi-astical courts carried on as it always had. In any case, there was little scope for development in the testamentary sphere, because the chapter on wills in the *Reformatio* said nothing which was new or different from what was already happening. Matrimonial causes were much more promising, as we shall see, but even Gibson recognized that the line taken by the *Reformatio*, on divorce in

---

[22] Ibid., V.3 (158), quoting *RLE* 20.16.
[23] Ibid., XXXIV.5 (850), quoting *RLE* 11.7.
[24] Ibid., XXII.3 (507), quoting *RLE* 8.4.
[25] Ibid., XIX.1 (453), quoting *RLE* 19.9.
[26] E.g., he mentions that Parliament had tried unsuccessfully to make parental consent for the marriage of minors obligatory, once in 1541 and again in 1689. See *Codex*, XXII.3 (507).
[27] *Haynes v Jephcot* (Mod. Rep. V, p. 168).
[28] Gibson, *Codex*, XXII.1 (499), quoting *RLE* 9.6.

particular, was no longer applicable, if it ever had been. It needed an issue where the existing law was unclear, but where the *Reformatio* offered an answer, to test its potential applicability. Such a case arose in 1792, when the Reverend John Hutchins, vicar of St Botolph, Aldersgate, brought charges against one of his churchwardens, because the latter had tried to prevent the use of chanting in the church, which he had authorized. In giving his judgment in the London consistory court, Sir William Scott (1745–1836)[29] had this to say:

> If then, chanting was unlawful anywhere but in cathedrals and colleges, these canons[30] are strangely worded and are of disputable meaning. But in order to show that they are not liable to such imputation, I shall justify my interpretation of them by a quotation from the *Reformatio legum* – a work of great authority in determining the practice of those times, whatever may be its correctness in matters of law. With respect to parish churches in cities, it is there observed: '*eadem parochiarum in urbibus constitutarum erit omnis ratio, festis et dominicis diebus, quae prius collegiis et cathedralibus ecclesiis (ut vocant) attributa fuit*'.[31]

What stands out in the above remark is Scott's estimation of the *Reformatio* as 'a work of great authority in determining the practice of those times'. He did not form that impression from Gibson, who, although he probably believed it, was far too careful to say so. More probably, Scott was dependent on another legal authority, William Salkeld (1671–1715), who had been a serjeant in the court of King's Bench from 1689 to 1711. In his well-known and widely used case notes, Salkeld claimed the following:

> Divorce for adultery was anciently *a vinculo matrimonii* and therefore in the beginning of the reign of Queen Elizabeth, the opinion of the Church of England was that after a divorce for adultery the parties

---

[29] He was a judge in the consistory court of London from 1788 to 1821, when he was created the first Baron Stowell and resigned his legal appointments.

[30] Scott means the injunctions of 1559, of which the forty-ninth is in dispute here. For the text, see G. L. Bray, *Documents of the English Reformation* (Cambridge, 1994), pp.344–5.

[31] *Hutchins v Denziloe*, 1 Hag. Con. 179 (*English Reports*, CLXI.518), quoting *RLE* 19.6, which says: 'The same pattern will apply in urban parishes, on feasts and Sundays, which formerly applied to colleges and cathedral churches (as they are called).' The date was 9 February 1792.

might marry again. But in Foljambe's case, *anno* 44 Elizabeth, in the Star Chamber, that opinion was changed. And Archbishop Bancroft [*sic*], upon the advice of divines, held that adultery was only a cause of divorce *a mensa et thoro*.[32]

Salkeld did not mention the *Reformatio* by name, but it is hard to see what other source he could have had in mind, and later generations assumed that he was referring to it. But if Scott was prepared to use the *Reformatio* in that way, he was more careful than Salkeld not to trespass into areas where such statements might be challenged. In the landmark case of *Dalrymple v Dalrymple*, for example, Scott pointed out that after the Reformation matrimony was no longer regarded as a sacrament by the Protestant churches, but despite the golden opportunity which this provided for quoting the *Reformatio*, or even Salkeld's judgment, he did not do so.[33]

This point must be borne in mind because of what happened next. In the first edition of his *Ecclesiastical Law*, Richard Burn quoted Gibson to the effect that Parliament had occasionally allowed divorces *a vinculo*, in accordance with the famous 'Matthaean exception' of Jesus (Matthew 19:9), as prescribed by the *Reformatio*.[34] But in the ninth edition of the same work, thoroughly revised and updated by Sir Robert Phillimore,[35] this information was supplemented by an extensive quotation from the *History of England* which had been published in 1830 by Sir James Mackintosh (1765–1832). Mackintosh there stated:

The articles on marriage (in the *Reformatio*) relate to questions . . . [which] affect the civil rights of all men, as well as the highest of all the

---

[32] 3 Salk. 138 (*English Reports*, XCI.738). For a discussion of the case *Rye v Fuljambe* and Salkeld's error concerning it, see the memorandum of Sir Lewis Dibdin presented to the Royal Commission on Divorce and Matrimonial Causes on 1 November 1910 and contained in its report, vol.3, pp.53–4 (see below for further details).

[33] 2 Hag. Con. 67–8 (*English Reports*, CXLI.670), 16 July 1811.

[34] R. Burn, *Ecclesiastical Law*, 2 vols. (London, 1763), vol.2, pp.40–1, referring to Gibson, *Codex*, XXII.17 (536) and *RLE* 10.5, 17. Gibson's chief evidence was the famous 'Parr case', in which the Marquess of Northampton, Lord Parr, remarried after divorcing his first wife for adultery. The marriage was declared lawful by a private Act of Parliament in 5–6 Edward VI (1551).

[35] 4 vols. (London, 1842).

moral interests of society. The book, not having received the royal confirmation, is not indeed law, but it is of great authority, and conveys the opinions of our first Reformers on problems which the law of England has not yet solved.[36]

That Mackintosh's view was not an isolated one can be confirmed by the testimony given to a select committee of the House of Lords on 18 March 1844 by Sir John Stoddart (1773–1856), who made the following remarks about the indissolubility of late Tudor marriages:

> The *Reformatio legum* had expressly broken in upon the principle, and would have been, in all probability, if King Edward VI had lived, the law of England. But although it was not the law of the land, it was the recognized opinion and sentiment of the English church, as I apprehend, at that time, because the *Reformatio legum* was drawn up by a sub-committee of eight persons out of the thirty-two nominated according to the directions of the act of Parliament, and at the head of those was Archbishop Cranmer; and therefore I apprehend that the *Reformatio legum*, having been published as a work of authority, although not of absolute legislative authority, it must have been, and in all probability was, followed, and that for that reason in the spiritual courts there were dissolutions of marriage, because I believe that from about the year 1550 to the year 1602 marriage was not held by the church, and therefore not held by the law, to be indissoluble. But in 1602 Archbishop Bancroft summoned together an assembly of divines, who were of opinion that marriage was indissoluble, though not upon the ground of its being a sacrament, but of its having, as Lord Stowell once described it, something sacramental in its nature. They held upon what I suppose to be sufficient authority of Scripture, that it was indissoluble, and then I apprehend that, in the same manner as Archbishop Cranmer's doctrine was followed down to 1602, the opinion of Archbishop Bancroft and the divines of that time has been followed to the present day in the spiritual courts.

Stoddart's historical reconstruction was demonstrably inaccurate, since it must have been clear to everyone that divorces *a vinculo* would not have been granted under Mary I (1553–8). He also repeated Salkeld's error regarding Archbishop Bancroft, who in 1602 was still Bishop of London and lacked the authority which Stoddart attributed to him. But in spite of these obvious blemishes,

[36] As quoted ibid., vol.2, p.503a.

nobody called Stoddart's opinion into question, and it was quoted as an authority both in the report of the Divorce Commission of 1853[37] and in the report of the Royal Commission on Divorce and Matrimonial Causes in 1912.[38] In fairness, neither Salkeld nor Stoddart claimed that divorce *a vinculo* was a written law in the sixteenth century. Their point was that it was then the generally held opinion of most leading divines, and that the church courts followed its theology, which meant that divorce *a vinculo* was valid even without being formally legislated. They were wrong to suppose this, but their authority carried all before it and issued in the Matrimonial Causes Act which received the royal assent on 25 August 1857. It was the *Reformatio*'s greatest triumph, because thanks to it, the reformers of 1857 could maintain that in providing once more for divorce *a vinculo*, they were merely fulfilling the wishes of the great Reformers of the Church of England, which had unfortunately been frustrated by Richard Bancroft in 1602.

The Second Death of the Reformatio

As often happens, it was at the moment of victory that the seeds of doubt and eventual destruction were sown. Edward Cardwell's edition of the *Reformatio* appeared in 1850, making it readily available for the first time in over two hundred years.[39] Cardwell wrote a preface to the work, making it quite clear that it never received the royal assent, and claiming that Queen Elizabeth I was quite antipathetic to it. Cardwell's view may be somewhat exaggerated and inaccurate in places, but on the whole it was correct and

[37] *First report of the commissioners appointed by Her Majesty to enquire into the law of divorce, and more particularly into the mode of obtaining divorces* a vinculo matrimonii (London, 1853), p.5. The commission was appointed on 10 December 1850, but in its report it incorporated material from the House of Lords' hearings held in 1844.

[38] *Report of the Royal Commission on Divorce and Matrimonial Causes* (London, 1912), Appendix I, p.18. The commission was appointed on 10 November 1909 and again (following the death of King Edward VII) on 21 June 1910. It submitted its report on 2 November 1912.

[39] Cardwell worked on the basis of the Foxe edition, but incorporated material from 1640 and from the draft MS (Harleian 426). He did not make a translation however. A translation of the MS has recently been published (J. Spalding, *The Reformation of the Ecclesiastical Laws of England, 1552* (Kirksville, MO, 1992) but there is still no critical edition or translation of the whole text.

was noted as such by John Keble in his pamphlet objecting to the
law of 1857.[40] Keble quoted extracts from the *Reformatio* and
claimed that they tallied with what Martin Bucer had written in *De
Regno Christi*, a work he had composed and submitted to King
Edward VI on 20 October 1550.[41]

This was subsequently picked up by Oscar Watkins, whose book
on the subject was referred to by the Divorce Commission in 1912.
Watkins wrote:

> The important collection of proposed canons known as the *Reformatio
> legum ecclesiasticarum*, by which it was intended to replace the ancient
> canon law of England, was exceedingly lax on the subject of divorce.
> Not only adultery, but desertion, continued absence, murderous enmity
> in the case of either party and also cruelty in the case of the husband,
> was held to justify divorce *a vinculo*, and to leave the parties free to
> marry again. Happily for England, the *Reformatio* never became law
> and is therefore only a historical curiosity.[42]

No one, not even Keble, had been quite as rude about the
Reformatio before, but despite Watkins's anti-Protestant theological bias, he was substantially correct on this point. When the
issue surfaced again in the Divorce Commission of 1910–12, the
church's big guns were ready for the attack. Sir Lewis Dibdin, Dean
of the Arches from 1903 to 1934, prepared a memorandum which
he read out before the commission at its hearing on 1 November
1910 and which he subsequently expanded for publication.[43] In this
he stated:

[40] J. Keble, *Sequel to the argument against unduly repealing the laws which treat
the nuptial bond as indissoluble* (Oxford, 1857), pp.201–4. Keble quotes *RLE* 10.5,
8–11.

[41] The relationship of the *Reformatio* to the *De Regno Christi* is complex,
although on this particular point it appears that Keble was probably right. See L.
Sachs, 'Thomas Cranmer's *Reformatio Legum Ecclesiasticarum* of 1553 in the
Context of English Church Law from the Later Middle Ages to the Canons of
1603', JCD dissertation, Catholic University of America, Washington, DC, 1982,
pp.105–16.

[42] O. D. Watkins, *Holy Matrimony: A Treatise on the Divine Laws of Marriage*
(London, 1895), p.426. He reproduces Keble's quotes from the *Reformatio* on
p.401.

[43] The memorandum is in the minutes of evidence of the commission's *Report*,
vol.3, pp.42–58 and the resulting book is L. Dibdin, *English Church Law and
Divorce. Part I: Notes on the* Reformatio Legum Ecclesiasticarum (London, 1912).

The conclusion seems to me to be inevitable that the *Reformatio legum* as we have it, so far as the section on divorce is concerned, is merely a literary relic representing the views derived from continental sources of certain individual churchmen of great eminence and influence. These views were no doubt also adopted by the rank and file of a section of extreme Protestants in this country, but except during a few years of Edward VI's reign, were never dominant in the Church of England. On the other hand, the opinion that adultery was on Biblical grounds a valid reason for the complete dissolution of marriage seems to have been widely, I should even say generally, held by English divines in the latter half of the sixteenth century.[44]

Sir Lewis backed up his opinion with a wealth of evidence never seen before (or since) on the matter, and it was impossible for the commission to ignore it, despite a feeble attempt to retain Stoddart's view as a viable alternative. But although Sir Lewis Dibdin could and did uphold the indissolubility of late Tudor marriage and discredit the *Reformatio* as evidence to the contrary, he could not ensure that a recognizably Christian doctrine of marriage would continue to be the law of the land. As the understanding of marriage and the grounds for divorce relied less and less on religious principles, the *Reformatio* ceased to be of any practical relevance. It had served a purpose in the run-up to 1857, because then it had allowed divorce reformers to remain within the umbrella of Christian teaching, even if that teaching had not previously been adopted by the ecclesiastical courts. But by 1910 those courts had long ceased to have any say in the matter. Divorce on many grounds was on the way, regardless of what any divines, living or dead, had to say about it. Within a generation it would be widespread both among the laity and among the clergy. The loose canons of 1553 had done their work, and when both church and society moved on to a new and unprecedented departure from traditional Christian standards of morality and behaviour, they were no longer needed.

---

[44] Divorce Commission *Report*, Appendix I, p.18, taken from the minutes of evidence, vol.3, p.52.

5

Ecclesiology, Ecumenism and Canon Law

ROBERT OMBRES

In 1956, Canon Eric Kemp set out to demarcate English canon law from secular law and to plead for its renewal. He argued that part of the specific identity of the law of the church comes from its dealing with the application of divine law and the preservation of the principles of church life which are found in the Scriptures, with the selection and ordination of the ministry, the administration of the sacraments, the conduct of public worship, and the outward pattern of the devotional life.[1] In 1987, the now Bishop Eric Kemp argued in similar vein that the subject-matter of the canons is as wide as the life of the church itself. At one end are matters fundamental to the church's existence such as the creeds and sacraments. At the other are practical arrangements such as the ownership and use of buildings.[2]

The word 'canon' is said by Bishop Kemp to have been used at quite an early stage of the church's history to denote both general principles governing the life of the Christian society and particular enactments of Christian assemblies. Moreover, until the middle of the nineteenth century, the ecclesiastical law in England was not regarded as an isolated system, but as a part, albeit with its own special rules, of a much greater system and one which might be illuminated and assisted by works of canonists in other lands.[3] In

---

[1] E. W. Kemp, *An Introduction to Canon Law in the Church of England*, being the Lichfield Cathedral Divinity Lectures for 1956 (London, 1957), p.76.

[2] E. W. Kemp, 'The Spirit of the Canon Law and its Application in England', *Ecclesiastical Law Journal*, 1 (1987–9), pp.5–14.

[3] Kemp, *Introduction*, p.62.

sum, both theology and history demonstrate the *ecclesiological* nature of canon law.

From these observations by Bishop Kemp on English canon law, prescriptive as well as descriptive, I should like to develop two aspects. Assuming that the law of the church is the application of its ecclesiology, then the resulting canon law will be affected by considering ecclesiology in the light of ecumenism. In other words, if a Christian denomination is committed to praying and working for the reunion of Christians ('ecumenism') then that denomination's theology of its nature and mission ('ecclesiology') will result in canon law of a certain kind. It will be argued that the canon law issuing from such an ecumenically minded ecclesiology will be both convergent and provisional.

That canon law is theological because of its sources, contents and aims has implications for all those involved in its making and workings. Bishop Kemp has consistently advocated the recognition of canon law's theological dimension. In the 1956 Lichfield Lectures he argued that those who are to be judges of ecclesiastical law should have a thorough training in it. By this he meant a real grounding in canonical jurisprudence, 'which of course includes more than a rudimentary knowledge of theology'.[4] Some thirty years later, Bishop Kemp remarked that the law of the church cannot be properly understood and properly administered without something more than a perfunctory knowledge of theology and church history.[5]

The argument to be advanced, concerning the link between ecclesiology, ecumenism and canon law, will be illustrated by drawing on Roman Catholic canon law. It is hoped, however, that ecclesiastical lawyers in the Church of England and other denominations will adopt the methodology suggested and carry out a similar exercise in terms of their own ecclesiology and law.

The use of Roman Catholic material in discussing English canon law should recall the impressively international and eirenic traditions of English ecclesiastical lawyers, continuing long after the Reformation. As Bishop Kemp has observed, no one can read the published reports of the cases in the ecclesiastical courts down to the middle of the last century without being struck by the

---

[4] Ibid., p.78.
[5] Kemp, 'Spirit of Canon Law', p.14.

familiarity of the advocates not only with the medieval canon law and its commentators, but also with the continental canonists of the sixteenth and seventeenth centuries.[6] Recent research on the practical writings of civilians from before 1640 has proved that they demonstrate that 'the Roman canon law' continued to exercise the predominant influence on shaping the King's ecclesiastical law after the Reformation.[7] It is indicative of the breadth and depth of the tradition which used to sustain English canon law that when the library of Doctors' Commons went on sale in 1861, the catalogue included:

> The works of the most celebrated English and foreign writers on civil, canon, and ecclesiastical law from the earliest times; a large collection of councils, synods, and decrees; works on church polity and discipline, monastic history and rule; . . . the works of the Fathers and Doctors of the Church, ecclesiastical historians and more recent divines.[8]

It will be argued, then, that if a Christian denomination derives canon law from its ecclesiology, and has a firm ecumenical commitment, then that law will strive to be both convergent with that of other denominations and aware of its provisional character. As this argument is illustrated from Roman Catholic canon law, one preliminary point of information is necessary.

The twentieth century has been the century of codification for the Catholic Church. Its principal canonical legislation is now found in the *Code of Canon Law* (1983) for the Latin Church, and the *Code of Canons of the Eastern Churches* (1990) for the twenty-one Eastern churches in full communion with Rome. The existence of different codes gives prominence to the plurality of

---

[6] Kemp, *Introduction*, p.62. For a striking example, one can read the non-consummation of marriage case of *Welde alias Aston v Welde* (1731) 2 Lee 580, heard before the Dean of the Arches, full of references to canonical and civilian texts and commentators, including decisions of the Roman Rota.

[7] R. H. Helmholz, *Roman Canon Law in Reformation England* (Cambridge, 1990), p.123. Helmholz concludes that the civilians quite obviously had no policy of excluding contemporary Catholic writers – quite the reverse in fact (p.146).

[8] G. D. Squibb, *Doctors' Commons* (Oxford, 1977), p.93. The report of the Archbishops' Commission on canon law, *The Canon Law of the Church of England* (London, 1947), p.57 noted how the judges and advocates in the ecclesiastical courts became people who naturally thought in terms of the traditional jurisprudence of the Church and not of the English Common Law.

constituent churches, and it also discourages mistaking the Latin Church for the universal Catholic Church. This dual codification is in itself of ecumenical relevance as establishing canonically within a single universal Catholic Church an ecclesiological multiplicity.

Canon Law as Convergent

Together with the need to discard a monolithic ecclesiology of the Catholic Church itself, since the Second Vatican Council (1962–5) we have also had to reconsider the relationship of the Catholic Church to other churches and ecclesial communities. The Council's decree on ecumenism, *Unitatis Redintegratio*, taught that those who believe in Christ and have been truly baptized are in some kind of communion with the Catholic Church, even though this communion is imperfect. The separated churches and communities as such have by no means been deprived of significance and importance in the mystery of salvation.[9]

In the Apostolic Constitution *Sacrae Disciplinae Leges*, promulgating the 1983 Code, Pope John Paul II emphasized the connection between ecclesiology and canon law. He said that the 'newness' found in the Second Vatican Council, and especially in its ecclesiological teaching, generated also the mark of 'newness' in the new code. Among the foremost elements which express the true and authentic image of the church is the assiduity which the church must devote to ecumenism.

If, therefore, renewed Roman Catholic ecclesiology makes ecumenism a priority then this must influence how its canon law is made, applied and understood. There are at least three important ways in which canon law should be affected by its derivation from an ecclesiology with marked ecumenical concerns.

Awareness of a Shared Heritage

Every Christian denomination should be actively aware of whatever common heritage it shares with other Christian bodies, and this heritage includes canon law. This heritage will be

---

[9] *Decrees of the Ecumenical Councils*, ed. N. P. Tanner (London, 1990), vol.2, p.910.

instantiated in significant councils, doctrine and teaching, canonical principles and concepts, practices and so on but most fundamentally, as the promulgating constitution of the 1983 Code states, it is necessary to remind ourselves of that distant heritage of law contained in the books of the Old and New Testaments. It is from this, as from its first source, that the whole juridical and legislative tradition of the church derives. Lyndwood's *Provinciale*, that monument of English canonical learning in an undivided Western Church, contains numerous scriptural references in its glosses.[10]

It was taught at Vatican II that Roman Catholics must gladly acknowledge and esteem the truly Christian endowments which derive from our common heritage and which are to be found among our separated brothers and sisters.[11] Of special interest in the context of English canon law is the conciliar assessment of the consequences of the loss of unity. Having dealt with divisions in Eastern Christianity, the decree on ecumenism (n.13) says:

> Other divisions arose more than four centuries later in the west, stemming from the events which are usually referred to as 'the Reformation'. As a result, many communions, national or confessional, were separated from the Roman see. Among those in which catholic traditions and institutions in part continue to subsist, the Anglican communion occupies a special place.

The retrieval of a common and formative heritage means that the study of the shared canonical past, a part of the more general theological and ecclesiological heritage, is to be pursued for more than antiquarian or scholarly ends. The retrieval of a common memory contributes to shaping our present Christian identity and specificity. An ecumenical ecclesiology is to be worked out at every level of a denomination, and for this task Episcopal Conferences in the Latin Church and the Synods of Eastern Catholic Churches can greatly facilitate effective ecumenical relations with the churches and ecclesial communities in the same area that are not in full communion. The most recent *Ecumenical Directory* notes how, as

---

[10] Lyndwood reveals his main sources when he says he cannot remember coming across a particular matter in canon or civil law nor in Scripture: *Provinciale* (Oxford, 1679), p.53c, s.v. *altari ministrat.*

[11] *Unitatis Redintegratio*, n.4 in *Decrees*, ed. Tanner, vol.2, p.912.

well as a common cultural and civic tradition, these Conferences
and Synods share a common ecclesial heritage dating from the time
before the divisions occurred.[12]

Knowledge of Other Canonical Systems

As well as exploring and taking possession of the shared canonical
heritage, a canon law derived from an ecclesiology committed to
ecumenism will also be aware of and influenced by the canonical
systems existing in other Christian denominations.

The exchange of gifts that is a mark of ecumenism begins with
acquiring knowledge of other Christian systems and goes on to
influence legislation, decision-making and the practice of canon
law in general. The 1993 *Ecumenical Directory* (para.107) is simul-
taneously encouraging and realistic:

> Catholics ought to show a sincere respect for the liturgical and
> sacramental discipline of other Churches and ecclesial Communities
> and these in their turn are asked to show the same respect for Catholic
> discipline. One of the objectives of the consultation mentioned above
> should be greater mutual understanding of each other's discipline and
> even an agreement on how to manage a situation in which the discipline
> of one Church calls into question or conflicts with the discipline of
> another.

The range of application of this principle is wide and pressing,
covering as it does such divisive canonical matters as the sharing of
Holy Communion, remarriage after divorce and the ordination of
women. In his encyclical letter on the task of ecumenism, *Ut Unum
Sint*, Pope John Paul II acknowledged that besides the doctrinal
differences needing to be resolved, Christians cannot under-
estimate the burden of long-standing misgivings inherited from the
past, and of mutual misunderstandings and prejudices. Com-
placency, indifference and insufficient knowledge of one another
often make this situation worse.[13]

The 1983 Code was formulated with ecumenism in mind, yet it is
more reticent than the 1990 Code for the Eastern Churches in

---

[12] *Directory for the Application of Principles and Norms on Ecumenism*
(London, 1993), para.28.
[13] *The Encyclicals of John Paul II*, ed. J. M. Miller (Huntington, 1996), p.915.

openly acknowledging the existence of other Christian juridical systems. To begin with, the 1990 Code differs from the code of the Latin Church in containing an entire section of canons on ecumenism (Title XVIII). Furthermore, its canons 780 and 781 explicitly refer to the law of other Christian denominations in cases of inter-church marriages and where the validity of marriages between non-Catholic Christians is at issue: the law of the Church of England comes within the scope of these canons.

From Comparison to Convergence

Legislators and office-holders in particular, if responsive to the ecumenical dimension of ecclesiology, should acquire the habit of constant and systematic comparison of their own canonical system with the juridical heritage they share with other denominations and with other existing canonical systems. Yet there is a further step – to advance from comparative canon law to converging canonical systems.

What is being proposed is that the canonical system of any denomination should take part in the general convergence that ecumenical advances bring about. In this vision, each canonical system will no doubt keep its specific characteristics but seek to maximize the compatibility of its canons with the church order of other denominations. Each canonical system will also attempt, to borrow a phrase from canon A8 of *The Canons of the Church of England*, to avoid occasions of strife. The ecumenical hope being expressed is not that one standardized canonical system will emerge from the reunion of Christians.[14] It is likely and desirable that each Christian denomination would retain some of its canonical traditions after reunion. Convergence means aiming even now at attaining canonical systems that are increasingly compatible and co-operative.[15]

[14] Although there is only one code for all the Eastern Catholic Churches, the promulgating Apostolic Constitution underlines that those who have legislative power in each of the churches must issue particular norms. The legislators must keep in mind the traditions of their own rite.

[15] G. R. Evans, *Authority in the Church: A Challenge to Anglicans* (Norwich, 1990); 'It is hard to say what constitute the non-negotiable fundamentals in matters of order' (p.138).

Canonists are now called to be comparatively minded in the way they understand and operate their particular church ordering. They need also to be active in promoting converging solutions to common legal problems, within the limits of fidelity to their own tradition in a still-divided Christianity. John Paul II showed remarkable and prophetic courage in saying: 'The increase of communion in a reform which is continuous and carried out in the light of Apostolic Tradition is certainly, in the present circumstances of Christians, one of the distinctive and most important aspects of ecumenism.' It is for canonists to accept this call and co-operate in increasing the degree of communion present amongst divided Christians 'in a reform which is continuous'. The Latin of the original text is even more forceful, echoing as it does the most divisive moment in the history of Western Christianity: 'Crescens in continua reformatione communio'.[16]

Canon Law as Provisional

It has been argued that relating closely the canon law of any Christian denomination to an ecumenically minded ecclesiology will make for comparison and convergence. If the already existing partial communion amongst the different churches and ecclesial communities is to increase, this can only come about under God's sovereign grace if there is an openness to change. In an important sense, canon law must be considered provisional.

Some elements in the total canonical system are unchanging because they express divine law or natural law, to use two convenient and traditional terms. But the understanding of even these unchanging elements is open to doctrinal development, and ecumenical dialogue has become an important feature of church life.[17] Much of any denomination's canonical system will not, however, be as unchanging. The temptation to be resisted here is to want to adopt what might be called 'the law of the Medes and Persians mentality' where it is inappropriate (see Daniel 6: 9).

[16] Ut Unum Sint, n.17, in Acta Apotolicae Sedis, 87 (1995), p.931. The concept of 'reformatio' was used in Unitatis Redintegratio, Vatican II's decree on ecumenism (n.6); in Decrees, ed. N. Tanner, vol.2, p.913.

[17] H. Meyer and L. Vischer (eds.), Growth in Agreement: Reports and Agreed Statements of Ecumenical Conversations on a World Level (New York, 1984).

It is in the nature of law to favour certainty and stability, and it has been suggested that canon law could well be an obstacle to ecumenism.[18] More specifically, it has been said that law has become an inadequate instrument in the field of ecumenism for two reasons. First, the complexity of the theological situation cannot be expressed in legal concepts. Thus 'separated brethren' means both to be divided and to be united, yet there are (at least for Roman Catholics) no legal concepts for partial communion. Secondly, the pace of development in ecumenism is too fast for legislation. Often enough, the best a canon lawyer can do is to weigh the values involved and see how the law can be adjusted to the legitimate postulates of the life of Christian bodies. Needless to say, anyone doing this 'weighing' and 'adjusting' should be as competent in ecclesiology as in canon law.[19]

These reservations about the place of canon law in the ecumenical movement are justified, but they should not be pressed too far because, not only for Roman Catholics, an ecclesiology without canon law is difficult to imagine even in ecumenical matters. This line of criticism should, however, encourage the practice of what John Paul II has called a *continua reformatio*, as well as instilling a sense of the provisional nature of much of the canonical system.

That canon law should be considered as 'provisional' is intended in two senses. It should be seen as provisional in being temporary, and also as exhibiting foresight. Apart from its immutable component, the canon law adopted at any particular time to express and reinforce a denomination's ecclesiology should be formulated and applied as appropriate to its age, combined with the greatest possible potential to facilitate future development. This will avoid some of the risk of canon law becoming in itself an obstacle to ecumenism. Making generous use of dispensations and permissions contributes to making canon law provisional.[20] So does ecumenically sensitive interpretation, for example of canon 1366

---

[18] B. F. Griffin, 'The Challenge of Ecumenism for Canonists', *Canon Law Society of America Proceedings*, 55 (1993), pp.17–38; T. J. Green, 'Changing Ecumenical Horizons: Their Impact on the 1983 Code', *The Jurist*, 56 (1996), pp.427–55.

[19] L. Örsy, *Theology and Canon Law* (Collegeville, Minnesota, 1992), p.59, n.6.

[20] A good example of the adaptation of the 1983 Code to facilitate ecumenism is *Mixed Marriages* (London, 1990), the revised Directory promulgated by the Bishops' Conference of England and Wales.

which provides that Roman Catholic parents who hand over their children to be baptized or brought up in a non-Catholic religion are to be punished.

In its deepest Christian sense, canon law is provisional in being for life on earth in view of everlasting life. Hence the reference in canon 204 of the 1983 Code to the church 'established in this world', and the programmatic statement in canon 1752 of that same code: 'keeping in mind the salvation of souls, which in the Church must always be the supreme law'.[21] The horizon of canon law, like that of the church, is not earthly history but the super-natural Kingdom of God. There have been, and are, several ways of understanding the nature of canon law and its functions. One of the inescapable tensions is that canon law shares some of the characteristics of secular law and some of theology. The law of the church is in part the result of the ordinary human impulse towards law-making and in part it issues from a divine ordering only disclosed to faith.

All law has to face the problem of mutability. If canon law is not understood and applied in a theological way, but is seen as simply the set of norms of a human society, then it will change according to social and political pressures and circumstances. Law appears then as an aspect of social engineering, one more instance of the general maxim *ubi societas, ibi ius*. If canon law is seen as theological, because it has supernatural sources and aims, then it will be created, understood and practised in specifically Christian ways.[22] All of this affects the nature and method of change in canon law, its provisional nature.

As it happens, both of the current codifications in the Catholic Church deal explicitly with the problem of fundamental change. The 1990 Code actually does so in the context of canon law and ecumenism. Once again, the codification of the Latin Church is less concerned with the impact of ecumenism on canon law than the codification of the Eastern Catholic Churches. This may be due to the fact that the Eastern Code, regulating as it does twenty-one distinct churches, is less prone to a monolithic view of itself than

---

[21] V. Bertolone, *La* Salus Animarum *nell'ordinamento giuridico della Chiesa* (Rome, 1987).

[22] R. Ombres, 'Canon Law and the Mystery of the Church', *Irish Theological Quarterly*, 62 (1996/7), pp.200–12.

the code for just the Latin Church. It may also be that the Eastern Code is more aware of the ecumenical pressures on canon law because the Eastern Catholic Churches are in a closer degree of communion with the other Eastern Churches than the Latin Church is with other Christian denominations in the West.

It is instructive to consider how the two current Catholic codifications see themselves in terms of change, that is in the light of their provisional nature. The *Preface* to the 1983 Code states that since the new law of the church lacks neither charity, equity, nor humanity, and is profoundly imbued with true Christian spirit, it has attempted to respond to both the external and internal nature given by God to the church. The document continues by saying of the new canon law:

> At the same time it desires to provide for the contemporary conditions and needs of the world. But, if on account of the very rapid changes which affect society today, certain imperfections in the law arise which require a new revision, the Church possesses such resources that, no less than in earlier centuries, it will be able to undertake the revision of the laws of its life.

This is a theologically impoverished account of the reasons which will necessitate large-scale change in canon law. It does firmly relate canon law to ecclesiology, going as far as speaking of 'the laws of its life', but any major revision is attributed to the rapid pace of change affecting human society.

This extract from the *Preface* to the 1983 Code of the Latin Church is in great contrast with what is said about the provisionality of the 1990 Code of the Eastern Catholic Churches. It should be stressed that both codes have equal dignity, firmness and juridical stability.[23] The contrast is in the account given of the factors that may bear on their mutability, their provisional nature. In *Sacri Canones*, the Apostolic Constitution promulgating the 1990 Eastern Code, Pope John Paul II said it was necessary for both codes to have the same firmness:

> That is, that they be in force until abrogated or changed by the supreme

---

[23] I. Žužek, 'Riflessioni circa la Costituzione Apostolica "Sacri Canones" (18 ottobre 1990)', *Apollinaris*, 65 (1992), pp.53–64.

authority of the Church for just causes, of which full communion of all the Churches of the East with the Catholic Church is indeed the most weighty, besides being most in accord with the desire of Our Saviour Jesus Christ himself.

The most weighty cause of major change put forward by the Pope (Christian reunion) would also alter the codification of the Latin Church. Yet it is of interest that the preliminary texts attached to the Latin Code do not mention this, and indeed offer a very different account of possible future causes of major canonical change. Related to this contrast between the two Catholic codifications is the fact that the Eastern Code gives a distinctive place to the canons on ecumenism, and it also explicitly refers to the canon law of other Christian denominations.[24]

---

[24] For further comparisons between the two codes see T. J. Green, 'The Fostering of Ecumenism: Comparative Reflections on the Latin and Eastern Codes', *Periodica*, 85 (1996), pp.397–444.

6

Bishops: Anglican and Catholic

CHRISTOPHER HILL

It gives me the greatest personal pleasure to contribute to this *festschrift*. A particular link between my subject and the person in whose honour these essays are written is that I was directly involved in Eric Kemp's consecration for the See of Chichester in Southwark Cathedral in the autumn of 1974. I had just taken up my post as Assistant Chaplain, Archbishop of Canterbury's Counsellors on Foreign Relations at Lambeth Palace – the old 'CFR' which then, as now under the newer guise of the Archbishop of Canterbury's Secretary for Ecumenical Affairs, inhabited the old laundry block at Lambeth. (It was T. S. Eliot who said that the difference between Anglicans and Roman Catholics was that we washed our dirty linen in public!) My post included responsibility for the Anglican Co-Secretaryship of the Anglican–Roman Catholic International Commission, and so for wider international Anglican–Roman Catholic relations. It also included some responsibility for the Old Catholic Churches. So I became involved in the invitation and arrangements for an Old Catholic co-consecrator to share in Dr Eric Kemp's consecration, he then being the chairman of the Church of England Conversations with the Old Catholic Church. This involved some complex signing of protocols and attestations which bore on the meaning and significance of episcopacy and the historic episcopal succession which, I suspect, would not have taken their particular form in the 1930s after the Bonn Agreement with the Old Catholic Churches had not Pope Leo XIII solemnly declared all Anglican orders 'absolutely null and utterly void' in 1896.[1]

[1] Cf. Christopher Hill on Old Catholic participation in Anglican consecrations in C. Hill, 'Anglican Orders: An Ecumenical Context', in R. W. Franklin (ed.),

This essay will look at some of the things that ARCIC (the Anglican–Roman Catholic International Commission) has had to say about episcopacy in its desire to move beyond the condemnation of Anglican orders by the Roman Catholic Church. It will also touch on Eric Kemp's own many-sided contribution to that debate and towards an ecumenical understanding of episcopacy and succession. Bishop Eric's contribution has been made in a number of ways: in the Anglican–Methodist Conversations; in the Anglican–Roman Catholic Joint Preparatory Commission (ARCIC's predecessor); through his chairmanship of the Faith and Order Advisory Group of the General Synod; through his membership of the House of Bishops, for longer than any other bishop; and through local ecumenical commitment with the Roman Catholic Bishop of Arundel and Brighton and Sussex Free Church leaders.

Apostolic Succession

It is also worth remembering that in seeking an acceptable ecumenical understanding and practice of episcopacy Eric Kemp's background was very much that of the last flowering and defence of the scholarly Tractarian understanding of apostolic succession. It was, after all, his own father-in-law who edited the last serious, sustained Anglican attempt at a scholarly justification for the absolute necessity of 'episcopacy in the apostolic succession' understood as the very *esse* of the church. *The Apostolic Ministry*, edited by Dr Kenneth Kirk, was published just after the end of the Second World War.[2] The most contentious emphasis of *The Apostolic Ministry* was its insistence on an historically provable unbroken chain of episcopal succession. The Methodist dissentients to the later Anglican–Methodist Scheme, led by Professor Kingsley Barrett, were quick to quote John Wesley on the incapability of historical proof of such a view of succession: 'a

Anglican Orders: Essays on the Centenary of Apostolicae Curae 1896–1996 (London, 1996), p.87.

[2] *The Apostolic Ministry: Essays on the History and the Doctrine of Episcopacy* (1946; 2nd edn. 1957).

fable which no man ever did or could prove'.[3] A rather different, interesting and more contemporary perspective on the 'historical continuity' thesis of *The Apostolic Ministry* is given by the distinguished Orthodox theologian Metropolitan John of Pergamon:

> The classical concept of apostolic succession has been formed in a one-sided way . . . As a result of this, the classical concept of apostolic succession has presented continuity in terms of historical process. Ideas of transmission, normativeness, etc. have become keynotes in this concept. Continuity with the apostles became inconceivable apart from the notion of a linear history. The problems that this one-sided approach has created hardly need to be mentioned. They are still with us today in the ecumenical dialogue.[4]

But if the unverifiable affirmation of an unbroken historical chain is not to be the starting-point for a rediscovery of an ecumenical episcopacy, where do we start? Eric Kemp has frequently stated – and I have heard this from him on several occasions, most recently in speaking about the present Anglican–Methodist report[5] – that ordination is always to be understood as the laying on of hands *accompanied by prayer*. The laying on of hands has no clear significance without a prayer of interpretation and signification. Sacraments are actions and interpretative words: the signs of the church are both visible and audible. The stress on ordination as prayer together with the laying on of hands was characteristic of the first series of Anglican–Methodist conversations of which Eric Kemp was a member. Was this drafted by him?

> In many New Testament contexts where it appears, the laying on of hands symbolizes the purpose of sharing with another some function, gift, benefit, or responsibility, which one has oneself received from God, and which God now wills to be passed on. It also expresses the self-identification and solidarity of one person, or group of persons, with another.

---

[3] Quoted in *Conversations between the Church of England and the Methodist Church: A Report to the Archbishops of Canterbury and York and the Conference of the Methodist Church* (London, 1963), p.58.

[4] J. D. Zizioulas, *Being as Communion: Studies in Personhood and the Church* (London, 1985), p.204. That Zizioulas has *The Apostolic Ministry* in mind is shown earlier in his argument by a direct reference and footnote, p.194.

[5] *Commitment to Mission and Unity: Report of the Informal Conversations between the Methodist Church and the Church of England* (London, 1996).

In the life of the Church the rite is regularly accompanied by prayer, which declares what it is that is being shared with, and desired for, the person on whom hands are being laid. This prayer is thus of the essence of the action, in which the laying on of hands itself has the significance of an outward and visible sign of the application of the prayer to a particular individual. In the Service of Reconciliation, therefore, the key to understanding the mutual laying on of hands (which is performed in silence) must be sought in the prayers which surround it.[6]

Equally, in the later ARCIC documents we find this characteristically Kempian emphasis on sound sacramental teaching:

This is expressed in ordination, when the bishop *prays* God to grant the gift of the Holy Spirit and lays hands on the candidate as the outward sign of the gifts bestowed. Because ministry is in and for the community and because ordination is an act in which the whole Church of God is involved, *this prayer and laying on of hands* take place within the context of the eucharist.[7]

I have emphasized this in the thought of Eric Kemp and ARCIC because 'the laying on of hands' is so often thought of mechanistically by both proponents and opponents of ordination within the catholic tradition. On the contrary, ordination is an act of the Holy Spirit at the prayerful request of the whole church signified by the laying on of hands by a bishop representing the apostolic continuity of his local church. It is a 'charismatic' event: meaning an event in which the Holy Spirit is present and active. John Zizioulas, whom I have already quoted, cites the Orthodox tradition as an important witness to the 'charismatic', 'Pentecostal', 'eschatological' and 'eucharistic' character of ordination. In other words God gives his presence through the Holy Spirit in the present; ordination is more a matter of 'presence' than 'pedigree'. He argues for a restored balance between the 'charismatic' and 'historical' emphases.

---

[6] *Towards Reconciliation: The Interim Statement of the Anglican–Methodist Unity Commission* (London, 1967), p.17.

[7] *Anglican–Roman Catholic International Commission: The Final Report* (London, 1982), p.37. Emphasis mine.

> Continuity here is guaranteed and expressed not by way of succession
> from generation to generation and from individual to individual, but in
> and through the convocation of the Church in one place, i.e. through its
> *eucharistic structure*. It is a *continuity of communities* and *Churches*
> that constitutes and expresses apostolic succession in this approach.[8]

The wisdom of this argument is demonstrated in the *episcopi
vagantes*. Here the Western over-historical emphasis in ordination
reaches its *reductio ad absurdum*.

Episcopacy and Jurisdiction

In 1967 Eric Kemp presented a paper to the Anglican–Roman
Catholic Joint Preparatory Commission, of which he was a
distinguished member. His subject was the less than snappily titled:
'What should be the minimum structure and essential life of the
local Church?' Characteristically, he began with the diocese as the
fundamental expression of the local church. The bishop is the
centre of unity for the diversity of Christians in his diocese. But
bishop, clergy and laity co-operate together in church government,
for ultimate authority lies with the whole body. Eric Kemp
criticized the then still-popular Roman Catholic distinction
between an *ecclesia docens* and an *ecclesia discens* as 'not con-
genial to Anglicans'. Finally, he drew attention to the major
difference in emphasis between Anglicans and Roman Catholics in
relation to the rights and independence of the local church. Not for
nothing did Eric Kemp have good friends among the continental
Old Catholics, who derived their orders from the archdiocese of
Utrecht at the time when 'centralist' Jesuit influence in Rome was
powerfully suppressing the local diocesan structure in the
Netherlands – in spite of those who became 'Old Catholics' having
suffered persecution under the Calvinists for continuing to adhere
to the catholic faith. Diocesan episcopacy led naturally on to a
consideration of the role of the Bishop of Rome in the universal
church. With prudential scholarly caution but also some proleptic
vision he concluded:

---

[8] Zizioulas, *Being as Communion*, p.177.

Most Anglicans would have no difficulty in giving the Papacy the kind of appellate jurisdiction assigned to it by the Council of Sardica. Where they would find difficulty is in being asked to acknowledge that the Pope has by divine commission the right to intervene with ordinary authority in the affairs of the local churches, to restrict their bishops in their pastoral office, or to suppress local hierarchies.[9]

It is worth noting in parenthesis that Eric Kemp clearly saw (and I think still sees) 'jurisdiction' as the real problem, rather than the more popularly perceived question of papal infallibility. With this ARCIC was later to concur. In its Agreed Statement *Authority in the Church I* (1976) the Commission listed remaining problems in ascending order of difficulty: the question of papal jurisdiction was placed last. Are there bishops in the church, or simply *one* bishop (ordinary)? The second ARCIC statement on authority admittedly did not follow that order; but this was more in response to responses to the original statement. In fact it can be argued that 'infallibility' is properly seen as an aspect of 'jurisdiction'. All jurisdictions have to posit a final court of appeal which must be presumed to be absolutely binding even if the confusing term 'infallible' is not used. The Sovereign in Parliament, for example, cannot be presumed to have made wrong law. Of course the law can be changed by the Sovereign in Parliament. The 'infallibility' or 'irreformability' of the decisions of a pope or council goes further in declaring that a particular law or decision cannot be changed. Then arises the logical conundrum of whether the designation of the 'irreformability' of a definition or decision is *itself* irreformable! Nevertheless, almost all Christians have wanted to say that certain Christian decisions cannot be set aside: the Canon of Scripture; the affirmation of the divinity and humanity of Christ; the Doctrine of the Trinity. As none of these three 'irrepealable' universal Christian decisions is found unambiguously or explicitly in Scripture, there has to be some ultimate structure for final decision-making. It is helpful to put the 'infallibility' question into such a wider jurisdictional framework.

The discussions which followed Eric Kemp's paper are instructive. An English Roman Catholic bishop, the late Dr

Langton Fox, criticized the way in which Canon Kemp saw the bishop as primarily the pastor of the local church. He saw ordination to the episcopate primarily as incorporation into an episcopal college succeeding the apostles. Ultimate authority lay with the episcopal college, which authority the whole church also needed to accept. The debate which followed encouraged Bishop Christopher Butler OSB because differences were found on both sides of the confessional divide. Reading between the lines I am sure Bishop Butler sided more with Canon Kemp. Constructively, a paper followed from the Oratorian Fr Louis Bouyer, a personal friend of Pope Paul VI. Citing Vatican II he too began with the local church as the basic manifestation of the Church of Christ. But the local bishop was not only the centre of local unity; because of his membership of the college of bishops, he was also the link of unity with the other churches. In this episcopal context the ministry of unity of the Bishop of Rome was also to be set.[10]

There is here an unresolved tension in Roman Catholic ecclesiology which will surface every time an ecumenical text touching on bishops, the local church, and the papacy is discussed. In Roman Catholic theology the tendency has traditionally (that is at least since the papal rejection of the Conciliar Movement, and the Counter-Reformation) given priority to the bishop's membership of the universal college of bishops, headed by the Bishop of Rome, over his attachment to his particular or local church. Since Vatican II theologians of the standing of Cardinal Yves Congar OP have argued conversely on biblical and patristic grounds. The question surfaces practically and traumatically in disputes over the appointment of 'Roman' bishops in Germany and Switzerland and in the disputed theological status of Episcopal Conferences *vis-à-vis* the central Vatican dicasteries. The distinguished pupil of Yves Congar, and a member of ARCIC, Fr J. M. R. Tillard OP has forcefully argued for the priority of the local church in communion with the other churches through its bishop and the ministry of the Bishop of Rome.[11] The last official salvo in this local versus universal debate was a letter from the Vatican Congregation for the Doctrine of the Faith, *The Church as Communion* (1992), signed by Cardinal

---

[10] Ibid., p.19.

[11] Cf. J. M. R. Tillard, *Église d'églises: L'Ecclésiologie de Communion* (Paris, 1987).

Joseph Ratzinger. While giving great importance to the local church (and its bishop) it nevertheless basically reaffirms a centrist view of the Church – moving away from, for example, ARCIC's position in *The Church as Communion* published only the previous year. Crucially, the clear teaching of Vatican II in *Lumen Gentium* spoke of the church (universal) existing in and out of the churches (local). The Congregation for the Doctrine of the Faith, in laudably wishing to avoid ecclesial federalism (communion thus becoming coalition), seems to reverse the Vatican II way of thinking by speaking of the churches (local) existing in and out of the church (universal).

Episcopacy and Ministry

ARCIC itself reached agreement on episcopacy in its agreed statements *Ministry and Ordination* (1973) and *Authority in the Church I* (1976), together with its *Elucidation* (1979) and *Communion in the Church* (1990). ARCIC spoke of the gradual emergence of a threefold pattern of ministry centred on the episcopate in recognized continuity not only with apostolic faith but also with the commission given to the apostles. This commission is one of *episcope* (oversight). Thus there is a distinction to be drawn between *episcope* and its forms. But this did not mean that ARCIC regarded as merely contingent the fact that *episcope* took the form of the threefold ministry centred on episcopacy. On the other hand there is nothing in the ARCIC documents which requires anyone to dismiss the possibility of *episcope* being found in the ministry of 'non-episcopal' churches. In this way the ARCIC documents are consistent with the earlier Anglican–Methodist Reports. In particular:

> We (ARCIC) both maintain that *episcope* must be exercised by ministers ordained in the apostolic succession (cf. para.16). Both our communions have retained and remained faithful to the threefold ministry centred on episcopacy as the form in which this *episcope* is to be exercised. Because our task was limited to examining relations between our two communions, we did not enter into the question whether there is any other form in which this *episcope* can be realised.[12]

[12] *Anglican–Roman Catholic International Commission: The Final Report* (London, 1982), p.43.

The meaning of apostolic succession here is defined in the original Agreed Statement:

> In the ordination of a new bishop, other bishops lay hands on him, as they request the gift of the Spirit for his ministry and receive him into their ministerial fellowship. Because they are entrusted with the oversight of other churches, this participation in his ordination signifies that this new bishop and his church are within the communion of churches. Moreover, because they are representative of their churches in fidelity to the teaching and mission of the apostles and are members of the episcopal college, their participation also ensures the historical continuity of this church with the apostolic Church and of its bishop with the original apostolic ministry. The communion of the churches in mission, faith, and holiness, through time and space, is thus symbolized and maintained in the bishop. Here are comprised the essential features of what is meant in our two traditions by ordination in the apostolic succession.[13]

It is worth underlining that such an understanding of apostolic succession never isolates the bishop from the church he represents. The apostolic succession of churches in doctrine and community is symbolized and maintained in the ordination of bishops.

ARCIC was also to be in full agreement with Eric Kemp's earlier paper about the bishop and the local church:

> The unity of local communities under one bishop constitutes what is commonly meant in our two communions by 'a local church', though the expression is sometimes used in other ways. Each local church is rooted in the witness of the apostles and entrusted with the apostolic mission. Faithful to the Gospel, celebrating the one eucharist and dedicated to the service of the same Lord, it is the Church of Christ.[14]

But the statement continues by arguing for the role of the bishop as the link of communion between local churches, and thus to the role of councils and synods, primacies and a universal primacy: all for the sake of the unity of the church and its mission. In a remarkable way the argument of ARCIC on authority was foreshadowed in the Preparatory Commission by the contributions of Eric Kemp and Louis Bouyer.

[13] Ibid., p.37.
[14] Ibid., p.55.

The Anglican Approach

Questions connected with the Roman primacy apart, the Church of England through the General Synod came to accept the ARCIC I Agreed Statements as sufficiently stating the Anglican view on episcopacy. The Resolution of the General Synod (1986) spoke of *Ministry and Ordination* as 'consonant in substance' with the faith of the Church of England. The Synod also recorded 'sufficient convergence on the nature of authority'. Voting in the dioceses had been more decisively in favour than in General Synod. Behind these synodical decisions lay a very considerable debate in which Eric Kemp again played a significant part. The Faith and Order Advisory Group of the General Synod, under Eric Kemp's chairmanship, had laboured long and hard, since the publication of the *Final Report* of ARCIC (1981) and the Faith and Order Commission Report, *Baptism, Eucharist and Ministry (The Lima Text)* (1982), on a considered and coherent Church of England response. This finally emerged in 1985 entitled *Towards a Church of England Response to BEM and ARCIC*. It was a substantial theological report of 109 pages. It made a significant contribution to the quality of the debate. In 1988 the Lambeth Conference also endorsed the ARCIC understandings of episcopacy in similar words to the Church of England. The careful and very full Church of England discussion, stimulated by the Faith and Order Advisory Group report, enabled the then Bishop of Bath and Wells, Dr George Carey, to see off a (small) minority wrecking amendment from more protestant-minded bishops suspicious of any agreement with Rome.

Since then Eric Kemp as a member of the House of Bishops has assented to a paper entitled: *Apostolicity and Succession* (1994). Though this statement utilizes material from the *Porvoo Common Statement* of the Anglican Nordic-Baltic conversations, it in many ways consolidates much that has gone before in Church of England ecumenical discussions about episcopacy and the apostolic succession of the church.[15] It represents a contemporary statement of the Church of England position on episcopacy and apostolicity. Many of its emphases are those which Eric Kemp has proposed,

---

[15] *Apostolicity and Succession*, House of Bishops Occasional Paper, General Synod of the Church of England (London, 1994): see especially pp.28–9.

particularly the role of prayer in ordination and the bishop as the representative of the local church of his diocese.

The most authoritative contemporary expression of episcopacy in the Church of England must however be found in the Ordinal of the *Alternative Service Book* (1980). Authorized after many of the major ecumenical documents referred to in this essay, it will not be unexpected that it should reflect the emerging ecumenical consensus on ministry and ordination, and on episcopacy in particular. In point of fact, however, the *Alternative Service Book* Ordinal has longer ecumenical antecedents and they also have links with Eric Kemp. A comparison with the draft Anglican–Methodist Ordinal[16] will immediately show a close and deliberate resemblance. But the story is more ecumenical and more fascinating than a simple adaptation from the draft Ordinal of the first ill-fated Anglican–Methodist Scheme. It was important that any Anglican–Methodist Ordinal had broad Anglican and ecumenical acceptance. So Eric Kemp was closely involved as a member of the Anglican–Methodist Conversations in the sharing of the draft Ordinal with the Roman Catholic Church. It was Louis Bouyer, whom we have already met, who gave a view from the Vatican that the draft Ordinal was acceptable from a Roman Catholic viewpoint – prescinding from the still debated issue of existing Anglican orders. In other words, and in rather old-fashioned terminology, used by a 'valid' bishop it would convey 'valid' orders.

The *Alternative Service Book* Ordinal therefore represents not only *the* official Church of England position on ministry and episcopacy, it also represents much of the ecumenical movement and much of the thought and work of Eric Kemp, Bishop of Chichester. Although the Ordinal naturally betrays its historical context,[17] we should therefore be prudent about its too wholesale revision as the Ordinal comes for scrutiny in the production of *Common Worship* for the Church of England in the year 2000 and beyond.

---

[16] Found in *Towards Reconciliation*, pp.54–73.

[17] Cf. P. Bradshaw, 'The Liturgical Consequences of *Apostolicae Curae* for Anglican Ordination Rites', in Franklin (ed.), *Anglican Orders,* p.75.

7

Consecration, Ius Liturgicum and the Canons

RUPERT BURSELL

Other than by reference to the actual services contained in the Book of Common Prayer itself there is little guidance as to what was intended to be embraced within the term 'common prayer'. There are no judicial decisions and textbooks are of little assistance.[1] The Latin text[2] of the 1603 canons used the phrases *precum publicarum* and *publicae liturgiae* to translate the English phrase 'of Common Prayer';[3] however, this interchangeability did not necessarily mean that every liturgy performed in public was also to be regarded as a 'common' prayer. This is important as section 2 of the Act of Uniformity, 1662,[4] laid down that: '[A]ll and singular ministers . . . shall be bound to say and use the morning prayer, evening prayer, celebration and administration of both the sacraments, and all other the public and common prayer, in such form as is mentioned in the said book . . .' The question therefore arises whether services, such as consecration of churches, might still legally be performed.

---

[1] See e.g., Halsbury, *Laws of England*, vol.14, *Ecclesiastical Law* (4th edn. London, 1975), para. 987, and R. D. H. Bursell, *Liturgy, Order and the Law* (Oxford, 1996), p.84, n.243.

[2] It was the Latin text that was authoritative: see J. V. Bullard, *Constitutions and Canons Ecclesiastical, 1604* (London, 1934), p.xvii; Halsbury, *Laws of England*, para. 308, n.1.

[3] Canons Ecclesiastical 1603, canons 14, 16 and 17 respectively.

[4] 1 Eliz. II, c. 2.

Consecration

The practice of consecrating churches is very ancient,[5] as is borne out by Gratian.[6] Moreover, that this was the law in England is confirmed by a constitution of Otho at the Council of London in 1237;[7] in addition, an Act in 1529 entitled 'Spiritual Persons abridged from having Pluralities of Livings'[8] permitted bishops to have six chaplains so that churches could be consecrated. Gibson's *Codex Iuris Ecclesiastici Anglicani*[9] and Phillimore's *Ecclesiastical Law of the Church of England*[10] – both of which cite Coke's *Institutes*[11] – confirm that this was indeed the law in England.

In fact within the Church of England the form of service of consecration was left to each individual bishop,[12] although a form of consecration was drawn up in Convocation in 1661 with the intention of including it in the new Prayer Book.[13] However, this was never authorized or published.[14] In either 1712 or 1715 a service of consecrating churches, chapels and churchyards was agreed by Convocation and was thereafter in general use.[15] Indeed, it was still in general use in 1938, although according to Cripps

---

[5] See, generally, E. C. Harrington, *The Object, Importance, and Antiquity of the Rite of Consecration of Churches* (London, Oxford, Cambridge and Exeter, 1847).

[6] *De cons.* D. 1 cc. 3 and 15.

[7] *Constitutiones Legatinae sive Legitimae Regionis Anglicanae D. Othonis, et D. Othoboni* (Oxford, 1679), pp.6–7. A constitution of Othobon in 1268 reiterated this requirement with additions: ibid., p.84.

[8] 21 Hen. VIII, c. 13, s. 24.

[9] Edmund Gibson, *Codex Iuris Ecclesiastici Anglicani* (2nd edn. Oxford, 1761), p.190.

[10] R. Phillimore, *The Ecclesiastical Law of the Church of England* (2nd edn. London, 1895), p.1383.

[11] 3 Co. Inst. 203.

[12] Harrington, *Rite of Consecration*, p.97. We know of at least eight different forms being used between 1610 and 1729: ibid., pp.97, 116–17 and 120–2.

[13] J. H. Blunt, *The Book of Church Law* (2nd edn. London, 1876), p.310.

[14] Harrington, *Rite of Consecration*, p.97. It was prepared by Bishop Cosin: Blunt, *Book of Church Law*, p.310.

[15] See R. Burn, *Ecclesiastical Law* (2nd edn. London, 1767), vol.2, p.298; R. Phillimore, *The Ecclesiastical Law of the Church of England* (1st edn. London, 1873), vol.2, p.1762; H. Cripps, *A Practical Treatise on the Law relating to the Church and Clergy* (8th edn. London, 1937), p.198. In fact the form of service set out by Burn is that of 1715: Harrington, *Rite of Consecration*, pp.115, 179 and 188.

'every bishop is left to his own discretion as to the form he might choose to observe in the consecration of churches'.[16] In 1957 Halsbury's *Laws of England*, having noted the necessity for consecration, went on to state that the bishop 'with such religious ceremony as he thinks fit' proceeds to consecrate the land and buildings.[17]

It is therefore clear that forms of consecration have been used continuously both during the Reformation itself and also since the Act of Uniformity, 1662; indeed, Cripps noted that the form of consecration even appeared in some editions of the Book of Common Prayer.[18] How, if at all, could this be legally justified?

It is, of course, always possible that all services of consecration were illegal as not having been prescribed within the Book of Common Prayer; thus it may be argued that the unauthorized Form of Consecration considered by Convocation in 1661 was omitted from the Prayer Book because any such service was regarded as unnecessary. However, this seems unlikely in the light of the regular use of such services. Rather, it seems better to look for legal arguments to support the continued use of services of consecration, although the question is differently answered by various textbook writers.[19]

Burn commented[20] that the form of service generally used, 'as it did not receive the royal assent, was not injoined to be observed'. In fact, none of the different forms of service received any such assent, although it is interesting to note that Burn felt the Crown could itself give such authorization.[21] Indeed, there were a number

---

[16] Cripps, *Practical Treatise*, p.198.

[17] Halsbury, *Laws of England*, vol.13, *Ecclesiastical Law* (3rd edn. London, 1957), p.395. Consecration, therefore, provides one of the rare occasions when it is possible to demonstrate that a usage of pre-Reformation canon law has been recognized, continued and acted upon since the Reformation. The procedural requirements of *Bishop of Exeter v Marshall* (1868) LR 3 HL 17 at 54–5 are therefore satisfied. See, too, *Re St Mary's, Westwell* [1968] 1 WLR 513, 1 All ER 631; Halsbury, *Laws of England*, vol.14, *Ecclesiastical Law* (4th edn. London, 1975), para. 307.

[18] Cripps, *Practical Treatise*, p.198.

[19] The one explanation not put forward is that of *de minimis*. This is hardly surprising, even if in the seventeenth century this legal principle had a wider ambit. After all, a service of consecration is not a mere variation but an entirely separate rite.

[20] Burn, *Ecclesiastical Law*, vol.1, p.298.

[21] See, similarly, Blunt, *Book of Church Law*, p.311.

of forms of prayers and services 'for the most part, publicly and authoritatively used during the reign of Queen Elizabeth [I]'[22] which were not set out in the then Prayer Book but which were certainly regarded as lawful.[23]

Walter Phillimore, however, felt some argument was called for. Not only did he stress that the 1529 Act had remained in force[24] but he continued:[25]

> Consecration services therefore rest, as originally all services rested, on the authority of the bishop. It is to be supposed (in the view of the editor) that either consecration services are outside the scope of the acts of uniformity, or that bishops (notwithstanding the decision in *Read v Bp of Lincoln*[26]) are, when officiating, outside its scope. Otherwise it would be difficult to find legal warrant either for these well established services or for those of dedicating sacred vessels, or bells, or lifeboats, or colours, or ships about to be launched.

In fact, Walter Phillimore had recently argued on behalf of the Bishop of Lincoln:[27] 'If a bishop is within the Acts of Uniformity then various modern services at which he officiates, services for the opening of churches, admission of deaconesses and others, are illegal.' However, the judgment of the court had been specifically restricted to services falling within the ambit of the Prayer Book:[28] '[T]he Court is of opinion that when a bishop ministers in any office prescribed by the Prayer Book he is a minister bound to observe the directions given to the minister in the rubrics of such office.' Indeed, the Act of Uniformity, 1662, section 2, embraced

---

[22] A. J. Stephens, *The Book of Common Prayer with Notes, Legal and Historical* (London, 1849), vol.1, pp.cv-cvi. The Queen also permitted 'nostra authoritate et privilegio regali' the services to be said in Latin in the colleges of Oxford and Cambridge and in those of Winchester and Eton: see A. J. Stephens, *The Statutes relating to the Ecclesiastical and Eleemosynary Institutions* (London, 1845), p.575, n.1. In the Act of Uniformity, 1662, this was specifically provided for by s.18.

[23] See, too, s.25 where 'according to the direction of lawful authority' meant '(according to practice) of the King, or Queen, in Council': see Gibson, *Codex*, p.280, n.(p).

[24] Phillimore, *Ecclesiastical Law* (2nd edn.), p.1391, n.(o). It was only repealed in 1817 by 57 Geo. III, c. 99.

[25] Phillimore, *Ecclesiastical Law* (2nd edn.), vol.2, p.1391.

[26] (1899) 14 PD 148.

[27] (1899) 14 PD 148 at 149.

[28] (1899) 14 PD 148 at 150.

'all and singular ministers in any cathedral, collegiate or parish church or chapel, or other place of public worship'. Unsurprisingly, therefore, Walter Phillimore did not attempt to argue against this (restricted) decision in the ensuing case of *Read v Bishop of Lincoln*.[29] Moreover, that this legal decision is correct is implicit in the latter case both at first instance and on appeal.[30]

The question of the legality of the services raised in argument both in the first case of *Read v Bishop of Lincoln* and in the text-book mentioned above, however, remained outstanding. Services of dedication of sacred vessels or, presumably, bells were likely to be performed inside a church and in public;[31] on the other hand, consecration of churchyards or services of dedication taking place other than in church, such as dedications of lifeboats, did not fall within the scope of section 2 and therefore were legal as long as the bishop retained a *ius liturgicum*.

The Act of Uniformity, 1662, section 3, spoke of 'all other the public and common prayer'.[32] However, the word 'common' had always appeared in the various Acts of Uniformity in addition to either 'open' or 'public'; as (presumably for clarity's sake) it was decided to alter 'open' to 'public', why did the word 'common' remain if it added nothing? If this argument is correct, the word 'common' necessarily added a different and distinct dimension to the ambit of the Act. In that case the word 'common' presumably meant 'of general application; general'.[33] If so, the Act of Uniformity, 1662, did not embrace services that were of an infrequent and unusual type.

Nevertheless, the argument in relation to forms of consecration of churches does not depend upon the meaning of the words 'public and common prayer'. As both Burn and Phillimore point out:[34] 'The law . . . takes no notice of churches or chapels till they

---

[29] [1891] P 9.

[30] [1892] AC 644, where the respondent did not appear.

[31] Dedication of colours may have taken place outside, unless the laying up of colours is referred to. Presumably a service of admission of a deaconess might take place in the bishop's private chapel or in church.

[32] The words 'in such form as is mentioned in the said book' most happily govern the forms of service to be used rather than the words 'public and common prayer'.

[33] See the *Oxford English Dictionary*. I am indebted to the unpublished Cardiff LL M essay of Mr P. L. S. Barrett for first drawing this possibility to my attention.

[34] Burn, *Ecclesiastical Law*, p.295 and Phillimore, *Ecclesiastical Law* (2nd edn.), p.1388.

are consecrated by the bishop.' This being so, the bishop could not
be conducting a service in a 'parish church or chapel, or other place
of public worship'. This is because the building did not become a
church or chapel until after the actual consecration. Such forms of
service therefore fell entirely outside the scope of the Act.

The Ius Liturgicum

As to the *ius liturgicum* the argument for its restriction depends
entirely upon the wording of the Acts of Uniformity themselves. In
so far as a service fell outside that wording it could not be so
restricted. In *Liturgy, Order and the Law* I argued (p.272) that:

> . . . even if there were such a *ius liturgicum* recognised in England, it is
> extremely doubtful whether it survived the Reformation. In order to
> have done so it must have been 'not repugnant contrariant or derogatory
> to the Laws or Statutes of the Realm' in 1534 when the ecclesiastical law
> was given statutory authority. Although not on the face of it contrary to
> the common law nor to the statutes then in force, it would have been
> contrary to the Act of Uniformity 1548 once enacted.

However, this seems to be incorrect. If they fell outside the Acts,
the legality of services of consecration may be demonstrated by an
appeal to that *ius liturgicum*, unless they can be justified by other
means.[35] On the other hand, the scope of any *ius liturgicum* was
still restricted by those Acts of Uniformity and a bishop could not
legally dispense with the requirements of the Acts or permit any
variations in relation to the services prescribed by them.[36]

---

[35] See J. Gainer, 'The *Jus Liturgicum* of the Bishop and the Church in Wales', in
N. Doe (ed.), *Essays in Canon Law* (Cardiff, 1992), p.116 *et seq*. Indeed, it is worth
noting that in *Rugg v Kingsmill* (1867) LR 2 PC 59 the Privy Council stated: '[the
incumbent's] argument appeared to extend so far as to question the validity of the
consecration of the Church by the Bishop. Their Lordships, however, see no reason
to doubt that the Bishop had full authority to consecrate this building.' See, too,
Sedgwick v Bourne [1920] 2 KB 267.

[36] *Read v Bishop of Lincoln* (1899) 14 PD 148. If the bishop is himself bound, *a
fortiori* he cannot permit breaches by others. It follows, for example, that a bishop
could not legally authorize the use of the Roman missal as that would have been
contrary to the prescription to use the Holy Communion service in the Book of
Common Prayer. As Gainer says, '*Jus Liturgicum*', p.120: 'There can be no doubt
that a bishop's liturgical authority includes the right to authorize services

Other arguments still therefore need to be considered. Cripps stated:[37]

> [A]lthough it might be unwise to depart from what has been prescribed by authority, and has in addition been sanctioned by custom, yet in our Church at the present day every bishop is left to his own discretion as to the form he might choose to observe in the consecration of churches.

In fact, this passage too is probably best read as an appeal to the *ius liturgicum*, especially as forms of consecration were never authorized by 'authority'. Even though one such form was approved by Convocation, that approval was never seen as amounting to a 'lawful authority'; indeed, even if that were not so, only that one approved service would have been so authorized. In addition, the bishops could not authorize themselves; a higher authority would have been required.

Custom

There only remains the question of custom. Cripps may, of course, have intended to refer not to a legal custom but, rather, to a mere practice or tradition.[38] Certainly the evidence indicates the continuous use of different forms of consecration.[39] Indeed, in so far as forms of consecration fall outside the scope of the Act of Uniformity, an appeal to custom adds nothing to a reliance upon the *ius liturgicum*.[40]

On the other hand, if they do not fall outside that scope, can they nevertheless be authorized by custom?[41] In *The Canon Law of the Church of England*, being the Report of the Archbishop's

---

additional to those in the Prayer Book. But the *ius liturgicum* does not extend to authorizing unilaterally services contrary to the Prayer Book or services which are already covered by the Prayer Book.'

[37] *Practical Treatise*, p.198.

[38] See Bursell, *Liturgy, Order and the Law,* p.5, n.28.

[39] However, the continuous use of different forms supports a practice more akin to the *ius liturgicum* rather than a specific custom to use a specific service.

[40] See n.53 below.

[41] See, generally, R. D. H. Bursell, 'What is the Place of Custom in English Canon Law?', *Ecclesiastical Law Journal*, 1 (4) (1989), p.12.

Commission on Canon Law[42] it was suggested that custom can abrogate a statute. However, this was written when the 1928 Prayer Book was being used in the church[43] and therefore at a time when it was necessary to justify that use if at all possible. In fact, the argument ignores decisions which are clearly binding within the ecclesiastical law. These lay down that statute law cannot be overridden either by usage or desuetude.[44] Moreover, in *Ridsdale v Clifton*[45] the Privy Council adopted the words of Dr Lushington: 'Usage, for a long series of years, in ecclesiastical customs especially, is entitled to the greatest respect; it has every presumption in its favour; but it cannot contravene or prevail against positive law, though, where doubt exists, it might turn the balance.' Thus, if the forms of service were indeed within the scope of the Act, custom could not make them legal.

The Position Today

Today, there seems little practical scope for the application of any *ius liturgicum* in the light of the provisions of Canon B4, paras 2 and 3:[46]

> 2. The archbishops may approve forms of service for use in any cathedral or church or elsewhere in the provinces of Canterbury and York on occasions for which no provision is made in the Book of Common Prayer or by the General Synod under Canon B 2 or by the Convocations under this Canon . . .
>
> 3. The Ordinary may approve forms of service for use in any cathedral or church or elsewhere in the diocese on occasion for which no

[42] (London, 1947), pp.66–7.

[43] See Bursell, *Liturgy, Order and the Law*, pp.273–9.

[44] See *Westerton v Liddell* (1857) Moore's Special Report 1; *Martin v Mackonochie* (1867) LR 2 A&E 116; and *Elphinstone v Purchas* (1870) LR 3 A&E 66. Gainer, *'Jus Liturgicum'* at p.119, n.23, seems to suggest that the permission by the Bishops of Wales and Hereford for the use of the Welsh version of the Prayer Book (1664) is an example of the *ius liturgicum* because it 'was not presented to Parliament nor was it annexed to the Act like the English version'; if so, it would have given a single example of custom overriding a statute. In fact statutory authority was given for this translation by s.27 of the Act of Uniformity, 1662, and the section does not require any such presentation or annexation.

[45] (1877) 2 PD 276 at p.331.

[46] Revised Canons Ecclesiastical (1969).

provision is made in the Book of Common Prayer or by the General Synod under Canon B 2 or by the Convocation or archbishops under this Canon . . .

However, in legal terms the question must arise whether, if the *ius liturgicum* survived in relation to services falling outside the ambit of the Book of Common Prayer, the exercise of that *ius* could permit a diocesan bishop to ignore, replace òr vary a form of service in the Book of Common Prayer or otherwise duly authorized.[47]

In so far as the Book of Common Prayer is concerned, the Church of England (Worship and Doctrine) Measure, 1974, section 1, enacts that the General Synod must ensure that 'the forms of service contained in the Book of Common Prayer continue to be available for use in the Church of England'. However, the relevant parts of the Act of Uniformity, 1662, have been repealed[48] and the authority of the Book of Common Prayer now rests upon the 1974 Measure and Canon B1, para. 1(1): 'The following forms of service shall be authorised for use in the Church of England: (a) the forms of service contained in the Book of Common Prayer'. The argument is, therefore, the same in relation to all the forms of service,[49] save that it gains greater force in relation to the Book of Common Prayer due to the express provision in section 1.

The canons which authorize all these forms of service are made pursuant to the 1974 Measure itself. Section 1(1) provides:

> It shall be lawful for the General Synod
> (a) to make provision by Canon with respect to worship in the Church of England, including provisions for empowering the General Synod to approve, amend, continue or discontinue forms of service . . . .

Moreover, section 1(5) further provides:

---

[47] N. Doe, *The Legal Framework of the Church of England* (Oxford, 1996), pp.289 and 293, refers to diocesan regulations which may purport to permit such a departure. Moreover, could a bishop now permit the use of the Roman missal (compare n.36 above)?

[48] Church of England (Worship and Doctrine) Measure, 1974, s.6(2), Sch.2.

[49] Canon B 1, para. 1(d)(e), both authorize the use of forms of service approved under Canons B 2 and 4.

Without prejudice to the generality of subsection (1) of this section, the General Synod may make provision by Canon

(a) for empowering the Convocations, the archbishops and the bishops of dioceses to approve forms of service for use on occasions for which no provision is made by forms of service contained in the Book of Common Prayer or approved by the General Synod or the Convocations under Canon . . .

It will be noted that these provisions are merely empowering; however, they are necessary not only as a matter of convention but also to authorize canons inconsistent with the royal prerogative or statute.[50] Norman Doe in *The Legal Framework of the Church of England* suggests that 'Unlike measures, canons do not (normally) have the same force and effect as parliamentary statutes' (p.72). However, the Synodical Government Measure, 1969,[51] is quite specific:

The functions of the General Synod shall be as follows:-
(a) to consider matters concerning the Church of England and to make provision in respect thereof
(ii) by Canon made, promulgated and executed in accordance with the like provisions and subject to the like restrictions and having the like legislative force as Canons heretofore made promulgated and executed by the Convocations of Canterbury and York . . .

Although the 1974 Measure provides for special majorities (s.3) and itself enacts the power to make the relevant canons, that does not mean that these canons have any different force from any other canon. .

In fact, any canon is binding on all the clergy in ecclesiastical matters[52] and, as such, binds a bishop as much as any other minister. Moreover, Canon B1, para. 2, specifically states: 'Every minister shall use only the forms of service authorised by this Canon, except so far as he may exercise the discretion permitted by Canon B 5 . . .' For this reason a bishop must himself comply with the canons in relation to worship and cannot authorize other

---

[50] See *Brown v Runcie* (1991) *Times* 20 February 1991; Doe, *Legal Framework*, p.73.
[51] S.2(1), Sch.2, art. 6(a)(ii).
[52] *Matthew v Burdett* (1703) 2 Salk 412.

ministers to depart from them.[53] Indeed, if this were not so, the continued use of the Book of Common Prayer would not be enshrined by the provisions of the 1974 Measure.

It therefore follows that, whatever the position was immediately after the passing of the Act of Uniformity, 1662, the *ius liturgicum* is necessarily now confined to the authorization of services in accordance with Canon B 4, paras 2 and 3, and to the giving of 'pastoral guidance, advice or direction' in accordance with Canon B 5, para. 4. Thus any broad *ius liturgicum* surviving in relation to services falling outside the ambit of the Book of Common Prayer has now been entirely abrogated.[54]

[53] Even though the authority of the various authorized services now depends upon canon rather than the Act of Uniformity, 1662, it cannot be argued that a contrary custom might now permit a departure therefrom. This is despite the fact that the *ius liturgicum* is merely an example of contrary custom: see Bursell, *Liturgy, Order and the Law*, p.271. Not only is this because of Canon B 1, para. 2, but also because, in the light of the Acts of Uniformity, it would be impossible to show that any custom against the use of authorized services survived the Reformation; moreover, the only pre-Reformation usage that can be demonstrated to have been continuous relates to forms of service to be used by diocesan bishops themselves: see n.17 above. The creation of the *ius liturgicum* itself predated the Reformation but only survived thereafter in a truncated form.

[54] *In re St Thomas, Pennywell* [1995] Fam 50 at 59B-E.

8

Church and State
in a Changing World

THOMAS GLYN WATKIN

The problem of the relationship between secular power and religious faith is as old as human society. In the earliest societies, there was clearly a belief that for the group to survive and thrive it was necessary for it to enjoy the favour of its divine protector, and that therefore any conduct which risked the loss of divine favour, on the part of the group as a whole or on the part of any member of it, had of necessity to be at the least suppressed and most probably punished. Retaining the favour of the gods was a key element in the formation of government policy, just as today democratic governments agonize over the retention of popular opinion, knowing that its loss may result in defeat at the next election.

In some ancient societies, elaborate rituals were devised to ascertain whether a particular course of action would be favoured by the gods. Among such rites was the taking of the auspices, for instance, in republican Rome, which, however much of a formality it became by the end of the republican period, had begun its course as an earnest attempt to disclose the wishes of the gods to men. It was to the College of Pontiffs that the Romans originally turned for the interpretation and clarification of their laws, much as Moses had been charged with dealing with difficult cases among the children of Israel, and for the same reason.[1] Such issues required for their effective solution a link between the human law-maker and the divine law-giver, the human function being to

---

[1] See *Digest*, I.2.2.6; Exodus, 18: 13–26.

enunciate for the benefit of the people what was pleasing to the gods. Even at the height of the empire, jurisprudence remained for the Romans the knowledge of things human and divine, a definition which came down to the medieval and modern world through incorporation in the legal compilations of the Christian emperor, Justinian.[2] If public opinion is to the modern legislator what the divine will was to his ancient counterpart, then in a sense the opinion polls which excite so much attention in modern politics are the equivalent to the taking of the auspices in earlier times.

The relationship between religion and the secular state to which such arrangements bear witness is one in which the state openly acknowledges that its success or failure depends upon divine favour. Moreover, there is also in both the Roman and the Hebrew dispensation a clear belief that that favour is not bestowed capriciously, nor is it withdrawn arbitrarily. If the human society lives in accordance with the divine will, then it will enjoy divine favour and prosper; if it transgresses that will, the favour of the gods will be withdrawn and the society in question will suffer.

Such a perspective upon human life might at first blush appear superstitious, even to those who hold sincere religious beliefs, although it is undoubtedly true that many would today perceive some of the problems facing the world, particularly with regard to issues such as global warming and environmental instability as being due, if not to divine disfavour, at least to human ignorance and negligence of living in accordance with the divine plan. It is perhaps therefore easier for this generation than for many in the past few centuries to appreciate the fears and concerns which underlay the view of the ancients in this regard.

It is against this background that the conversion of Constantine and his subsequent activity in relation to the church should be viewed. In terms of the traditional Roman beliefs in the need for divine favour to prosper human endeavour and the availability of signs to make manifest such favour, Constantine's experience before the battle of the Milvian Bridge would have been a potent indicator of which faith he should follow not just for his own sake but also for that of the empire. His subsequent determination to resolve conflicts within the church by summoning councils to settle contentions can also be seen as expressions of imperial concern

---

[2] *Digest*, I.1.10.2; Justinian, *Institutes*, I.1.1.

that there should be no departure from the will of God in the practice and belief of the faith which was now that of the emperor and which was to become before the end of the fourth century the official religion of the empire itself.

This absorption of the Christian faith and the church into the state by the Roman authorities was bound to transform the relationship between the secular and the sacred. For the first time, secular government and ecclesiastical authority existed side by side as partners in the later empire. The church was able to make use of the structures of imperial government as reformed by Diocletian at the end of the third century to shape its own territorial and hierarchical arrangements, which were destined to survive the waning of Roman power in western Europe. Long after the Goths, the Lombards and the Franks had overrun the lands of the western empire, the church retained its seat of government at Rome and organized itself according to the erstwhile imperial pattern of provinces, dioceses and vicariates. Alongside the territorial expression of its authority, its bishops continued to exercise as under the Christian emperors jurisdiction over the affairs of the faithful, holding tribunals to adjudicate their disputes and administering justice in broad conformity with Roman legal ideals. *Ecclesia vivit lege romana.* The Roman law of property, which had originally upheld the view that property dedicated to sacred or religious purposes was for ever removed from the possibility of private ownership, was adapted to provide for gifts to the purposes of Jesus Christ and his saints.[3]

During the centuries following the fall of the Roman empire in the west, the church constituted without doubt the most sophisticated and learned institution in western Europe, and thus able to wield considerable influence, if not power, in secular affairs. The history of the Lombard kingdom of Italy bears witness to an immediate increase in ecclesiastical privilege once the rulers were converted from Arian to Catholic Christianity.[4] The church and its ministers are regularly accorded high status in the laws of the Germanic peoples following their conversion, and the skills of literacy and administration which the churchmen brought with

---

[3] See Carlo Calisse, *A History of Italian Law* (Boston, 1928; New York, 1969), pp.121–3.

[4] Especially under Liutprand, 713–35; see Carlo Calisse in *A General Survey of Continental Legal History* (Boston, 1912, New York 1968) pp.23–4.

them were obviously greatly prized.[5] The capitularies of Charlemagne and his successors in the ninth century bear witness to a concentrated endeavour to direct legal development in a Christian, that is a canonical, direction.[6] The same had been true under the later Roman emperors, who had struggled valiantly to promote ecclesiastical policies in such unpopular areas as forbidding the exposure of new-born children and upholding the life-long nature of marriage by restricting the availability of repudiation and consensual divorce.[7]

The fall of the Roman empire in the west had however ended the coexistence of church and state in western Europe. As the new Europe first of tribes and later of feudal lordships developed, the church occupied a unique and powerful position, in that it had a role in all of these areas and was subservient to none of them. The failure of the Carolingian empire left the church free to develop its own view of government and legality which it could then seek to introduce into the territories of Christian rulers by virtue of its canonical authority and by dint of its essential usefulness to secular rulers. The Europe of the eleventh, twelfth and thirteenth centuries was a Europe of lordships and not of states, and the church, through its assertion of the ecclesiastical lordship of the pope, was able to compete on remarkably equal terms in power struggles with the secular rulers.

This was the age of the great lawyer popes, such as Gregory VII and Innocent III. It was the age in which, following the revival of Roman law studies at the Italian universities, the church developed its own system of canon law, which excelled the legal arrangements of the secular powers both in learning and sophistication. It was also the age in which a hierarchical structure of courts culminating in the pope's own curia at Rome offered to the faithful the legal services of the church in open competition with those of the feudal and even monarchical governors. The church had become a power independent of princes, threatening to exercise jurisdiction over them in a manner perhaps reminiscent of supra-national bodies such as the United Nations in our own day.[8]

---

[5] The Early English laws of Aethelbehrt furnish an interesting example.

[6] See Calisse, *General Survey*, pp.36–7.

[7] See J. A. C. Thomas, *A Textbook of Roman Law* (Amsterdam, 1976), pp.414–15, 426–7.

[8] See, for instance, I. S. Robinson, *The Papacy 1073–1198* (Cambridge, 1990).

The confrontations which this approach engendered, from the Investiture Contest on the continent to the Becket controversy at home, ended in the church having to settle for a restricted role in the life of Europe's emerging nations, a role which varied from country to country. It still, however, managed to police the boundary between secular law and the divine will, both as revealed in Scripture and through the natural law made manifest by reason. As well as administering canon law in its own courts, the church influenced the development of secular legal orders. In the north of France, for instance, where people continued to live according to the customs of their own localities, the church acquired the right to adjudicate upon the acceptability of customary rules according to their congruence with divine law and reason.[9] In England, the Court of Chancery developed as a court of conscience, supplementing and correcting the common law administered in the King's other courts, the Chancellor, being an ecclesiastic, deriving many of his principles either directly or indirectly from canonical learning.[10]

As the feudal monarchies of the high Middle Ages were gradually transformed into the Renaissance states of early modern Europe, so the church found itself for the first time face to face with rulers who desired absolute political power within their territories on all matters. To such rulers, the Reformation must have been a god-send, for the challenge which it offered to the authority of the Western Catholic Church gave respectability and legitimacy to their claims to be the sole arbiters within their lands even on religious issues. By discrediting the claims of the papacy to universal ecclesiastical hegemony, the Reformation left the field open for the secular rulers to claim that they alone were answerable before God for the good governance of their respective kingdoms, and that neither outside influences, such as the church, nor the wishes of their subjects within their realms had any part to play in government. *Cuius regio, eius religio* summed up the new relationship between ruler and religion in much of Europe. The choice between rival versions of the Christian faith was for the secular prince to make, and it was the duty of his subjects to respect and

[9] See J. B. Brissaud in Calisse, *General Survey*, p.218.

[10] See R. H. Helmholz, 'The Early Enforcement of Uses', *Columbia Law Review*, 79 (1979), p.1503; reprinted in Helmholz, *Canon Law and the Law of England* (London and Ronceverte, 1987), pp.341–2.

support his choice in matters of religion as much as in other matters of state.

The origins of the Church of England are firmly rooted in this approach. To be a subject of the King of England entailed acceptance of the reformed faith as part and parcel of loyalty to the sovereign. Although late seventeenth-century England was to be in the vanguard of those states which introduced a measure of tolerance in matters of religion, nevertheless the Church of England was the church of the King's subjects and any other arrangement, though tolerated, was the exception not the rule. The King was supreme governor of the church within his realms, and to challenge his authority was therefore an offence to the God whose vicegerent he was on earth, and to challenge his faith was also a challenge to his right to rule and therefore savoured of sedition.

Here we find the second main approach to the relationship of state and church, namely that which sees them entirely intertwined, not because divine favour is essential for successful secular government, but because the King is God's representative upon earth and is alone accountable to God for the manner in which he governs. Loyalty and disloyalty to the King necessarily involves faith or lack of faith in God and vice versa. The nation-state has become the context in which all the important acts of life take place. No longer is there an outside institution which has a claim upon the allegiance of the faithful in matters of religion. Even in Catholic countries, such as France, resistance to the directives of the Pope of Rome was firm; the decrees of the reforming Council of Trent were only introduced into the French king's domains as and when he thought fit and by means of royal ordinance.[11]

The emergence of a Europe of nation-states placed the church as an institution at a disadvantage. No longer could the Church deal on an equal footing with the territorial rulers of western Christendom. Unsurprisingly, in the same way as the church had sought a feudal overlordship over the kingdoms of Europe in earlier centuries, so in the early modern period, the Papal States emerge in central Italy as a territorial power base for the papacy, enabling it to deal on something like equal terms with the other princes of Christendom.

The emergence of nation-states produced alongside national

---

[11] Such as the *Ordonnance* of Blois (1579) regulating the form of marriage.

churches the phenomenon of national legal systems. Whereas previously the learned law had been that taught in the civil and canon-law faculties of the universities, having an existence which transcended territorial boundaries, nation-states developed national laws. Although it was not until the eighteenth and nineteenth centuries that this development finally undermined the existence of a European *ius commune*, in matters of procedure and jurisdiction the process began in the sixteenth century. In that the church's canon law had played an important part in the shaping of the *ius commune*, its demise further reduced the influence of the church in secular government. The legal codifications of the nineteenth century sought to supply all the legal needs of the peoples those codes served. The legal systems set up to administer the laws contained in those codes offered little space for the ecclesiastical tribunals which had operated in earlier centuries other than regarding the discipline of the clergy.

The main thrust of the legal reforms of the late eighteenth and early nineteenth centuries however was the attack upon royal absolutism. The philosophical concept of the social contract postulated that men and women enjoyed basic human rights which human societies such as the state existed to recognize and protect, but which were not created by the legal orders of those states. Such fundamental rights included liberty of conscience in matters of religious belief, so that for the social-contract theorists whose writings inspired the constitutions produced as a result of the American and French Revolutions, the function of the state and of rulers was to protect and promote the fundamental rights of citizens. Gone therefore was any notion of religion being a matter solely for the ruler to decide; faith was now a matter for the individual, and the ruler's role was to protect the individual's freedom of choice. This is the perspective of most modern constitutions upon religious belief. No longer is the ruler the arbiter and defender of his people's faith; he is more a defender of faith in the abstract, as suggested of late by the Prince of Wales in a remark which appears as bizarre to an English audience as it must appear a constitutional commonplace to the citizens of most continental countries.

Even in England, the nineteenth century saw the clear emergence of a concept of the state based upon individual rights. Religious disabilities were gradually removed. Dissenters and Roman Catholics, and even non-Christians including those of other faiths, such as Jews, and those of no faith at all, were permitted to matriculate at the universities and to stand for election to parliament.[12] Membership of the national church was no longer a requirement for full citizenship. This inevitably meant that it could hardly remain proper for the church to be governed by bodies which were no longer composed of its members, the idea of being a member of the church as a distinct concept from being a citizen of the country being a result of the new perception of religious freedom as an individual right. Likewise, the state was forced to reconsider the role of the church and canon law in the life of the nation and its people. It could no longer demand that all citizens should marry according to the rites of the church, nor that the courts of the church should have exclusive jurisdiction over matrimonial causes and the testamentary dispositions of the populace. Accordingly, civil marriage ceremonies were devised as an alternative to marriage according to the rites of the established church, and provisions were made to allow Dissenters to marry in their own places of worship according to their own ceremonies, provided that a basic legal minimum was present. In 1857, probate and matrimonial causes were transferred to the jurisdiction of newly established state courts, and divorce *a vinculo matrimonio* became a possibility by judicial decree.[13]

If England was in effect recognizing that religious faith is a matter of choice and that that choice is a fundamental human right which states exist to protect not to determine, then the question arises as to where this leaves a national church. The problem is not England's alone. In all those countries which followed, at the Reformation and after the Peace of Westphalia in 1648, the principle *cuius regio, eius religio*, the shift from a ruler-chosen faith to an individually selected creed posed the same dilemma. The matter was further complicated during the nineteenth century as growing dissatisfaction was aired at what was perceived to be the over-individualistic approach to rights manifested by the legislation enacted in the wake of the French Revolution. In Germany in particular, where many institutions of a corporate nature were part of the endemic legal tradition, there was a resurgence of feeling

[12] See, for instance, the Universities Tests Acts 1871 and the Parliamentary Oaths Act 1866.

[13] See the Matrimonial Causes Act 1857 and the Court of Probate Act 1857.

that rights pertained not only to individuals but also to groups or associations, ranging from the family through local communities and trade confederations and trade unions to the state itself. Religious associations clearly constituted one such grouping, and modern constitutions, in countries which have written constitutions, generally recognize the duty of the state to protect and promote not just the rights of its individual citizens but also the interests of such subjunctive associations. Again, even in England, such developments occurred in the nineteenth century. It would scarcely have been sufficient to allow individuals to choose to be Roman Catholics or Nonconformists if the law did not enable them to associate for purposes of worship and the owning of property and goods in furtherance of their beliefs. Once that step was taken, it was bound to lead to the question of why one such group should enjoy a privileged position under the law by reason only that it had been historically the ruler's choice of church for his kingdom in an age when freedom of choice in matters of faith was not recognized by the law. In Wales, this question was a burning issue during the second half of the nineteenth century and culminated in the disestablishment of the Church of England within Wales in 1920.

It is not only the privileges of establishment which can give rise to resentment. The link between a church and the state within which it functions can also be productive of tensions. With states now seeing themselves as existing for the protection of the rights of their citizens, with those citizens having the inalienable right to make up their own minds on matters of conscience, difficulties result for such churches in reconciling their role as a part of such a value-free polity with their clear duty to witness to the values of the Gospel. The Church of England, for example, has faced this dilemma on diverse issues, ranging from the ordination of women, where the state's commitment to sexual equality conflicts with the resistance of many to the admission of women to the ordained ministry, to matters of sexual morality, where increasing pressure to grant equal rights to groups such as homosexuals appears to some to be in direct conflict with biblical teaching on the subject. The reception of the European Convention on Human Rights into the domestic law of the United Kingdom may exacerbate matters further. If, for instance, the state feels obligated to accept homosexual unions as forms of marriage, while it is one thing for a non-established church to refuse to solemnize such weddings, it is another for a church which is part of the state to refuse. In effect, a state organ is then refusing.

It is interesting that this problem is more acute in those countries which adopted the principle of *cuius regio, eius religio* in the wake of the Protestant Reformation. The Roman Catholic Church has avoided some of these pressures because its established seat of government is a nation-state in its own right. The creation of the Vatican City State in 1929 allowed the Roman Catholic Church to treat with other states on an equal legal footing.[14] It has therefore been able to enter into Concordats with other countries, setting up treaty relations with them which are binding in international law. Thus, in Italy, for instance, the state's divorce laws recognize that divorce decrees only terminate the civil effects of marriage, allowing the churches complete freedom with regard to their response. The church is seen as an association or corporate body which has fundamental rights of its own, and whose liberty of conscience must be respected. Likewise, the clergy are recognized as being subjects of the church's canon law, so that in the event of a conflict between the domestic law of the state and the canon law of the church, such a conflict has to be resolved by use of the principles of private international law. Thus, for instance, decrees of nullity issued by the church courts have to be recognized by the state in its courts according to these principles before being accepted by the domestic law.

Such freedom is clearly not available to churches which are part of a state or established by law. Yet, there is currently a discernible trend for other entities, such as multinational corporations, to seek the capacity to enter into treaty relations with nation-states. Indeed, there is evidence that as supra-national relations develop, as within the European Union, global life is becoming less international and more inter-institutional, resulting in the need for legal arrangements which buttress individual and group rights across, rather than within, national boundaries. Throughout its history, the church has responded to changes in the social and political outlook of the peoples to whom it ministers by adapting its own structures to enable it to function effectively in the world. One

[14] See T. G. Watkin, *The Italian Legal Tradition* (London 1997), pp.50, 82 and 170.

could hardly expect less of a church which witnesses to the Incarnation of its Lord. As one looks to the emerging social and political order of the new millennium, with increasing globalization, it is clearly going to be necessary for the church once more to adapt its structures to changing and changed circumstances. It has never failed to meet this challenge in the past, and there are signs that it is, as usual, in the vanguard of such change. There are reasons for believing that in the new European and world order, national or established churches are destined to become anachronisms.

9

Ecclesiastical Quasi-Legislation

NORMAN DOE

In 1957 Eric Kemp wrote that the 'ancient inheritance of the Church's jurisprudence' embraces two views of canon law: one stresses its hard side – some canons are coercive and mandatory; the other its soft side – some canons are exhortatory, consisting of standards which 'the Church thought ought to be observed but was not prepared to enforce by action at law'.[1] In 1995 the Turnbull Commission proposed an associated idea: the church should seek 'legislation that was less prescriptive and detailed, giving more discretion to dioceses and those in day-to-day charge of . . . the Church's work to apply it in ways which best suit their local circumstances'.[2] For both, the church should be characterized by arrangements which allow for less formal methods of ecclesiastical regulation. Of course, the Church of England is regulated by many forms of primary and secondary legislation – measures, canons, schemes and other instruments created under synodical measures. They exist to command, to prohibit and to permit. But these are not the only sources of ecclesiastical regulation. Regulation is increasingly being effected by means of what may be described as *ecclesiastical quasi-legislation* – extra-legal regulatory instruments informally made by a wide range of church bodies.[3]

[1] E. W. Kemp, *Introduction to Canon Law in the Church of England* (London, 1957), pp.81–2.

[2] *Working as One Body*, Report of the Archbishops' Commission on the Organization of the Church of England (London, 1995), para. 6.40.

[3] I am grateful to the English Clergy Association for permission to reproduce substantial extracts from a published version of papers delivered in London in 1996 appearing in *Parson and Parish*, 147 (1996), p.8; I am also indebted to responses given to a lecture on this subject for Cardiff Canon Law graduates at a meeting organized by Mark Hill and held at St Anne's Church, Soho, in March 1996.

Quasi-Legislation in Secular Jurisprudence

Secular jurisprudence distinguishes *imperium*, the use by government of coercive power, and *dominium*, the use of persuasive power.[4] Secular government employs formal law to coerce results, and quasi-legislation to persuade results.[5] Government departments commonly make rules to regulate the exercise of statutory or other discretionary powers. The underlying rationale is to ensure consistency and public confidence in decision-making. This quasi-legislation, expressed in the form of broad principles, standards, circulars, guidelines or codes of practice,[6] may contain procedures and prescriptions about official conduct or guidance on how to interpret legislation. However, there are limits on what may be achieved by quasi-legislation: 'quasi-legislation does not (indeed cannot) effect alterations in statute or common law but . . . it can affect private interests and may have legal consequences'.[7] It has been decided judicially that government cannot override a statutory discretion by issuing guidelines as to how the power is to be used or by treating guidance as binding. Similarly, interpretation of laws in a circular will have no legal authority, though they may acquire 'vitality and strength' by being accepted and acted upon. If a person's interests are adversely affected by a departmental interpretation, that person may obtain a declaration that the interpretation is wrong in law. Indeed, there is considerable agreement that the dangers with quasi-legislation are as follows: it constitutes rule-making which bypasses Parliament; often a clear legal pedigree is uncertain; it is often couched in imprecise language; and it allows judges to be instructed by ministers and departments on the meaning of law.[8]

[4] R. E. Megarry, 'Administrative Quasi-Legislation', *Law Quarterly Review*, 60 (1944), p.125, and G. Ganz, *Quasi-Legislation: Recent Developments in Secondary Legislation* (London, 1987).

[5] T. Daintith, 'Legal Analysis of Economic Policy', *Journal of Law and Society*, 9 (1982), p.191.

[6] E.g. Employment Act 1980: the minister may issue codes of practice, 'practical guidance . . . promoting . . . industrial relations', which, in legal proceedings, 'shall be admissible in evidence' and 'shall be taken into account'; the code must have parliamentary approval.

[7] C. Turpin, *British Government and the Constitution: Text, Cases and Materials* (2nd edn. London, 1990), p.355.

[8] For judicial decisions in support of these propositions, see R. Baldwin and J. Houghton, 'Circular Arguments: The Status and Legitimacy of Administrative Rules', *Public Law* (1986), p.239.

The Church's Use of Quasi-Legislation

With informal rule-making, generally, the church follows the state. Alongside formal law, synodical measures and canons, exist instruments containing rules, responsibilities, standards and norms which are not made as a result of formal legislative processes. These *dominium* instruments include 'policy documents', 'regulations', 'directions', 'codes of practice', 'circulars', 'guidance' or 'guidelines' or other documents issued centrally or at diocesan level – by the Standing Committee of General Synod, the House of Bishops, the Church Commissioners and diocesan bishops, with or without the agreement of their diocesan synods.[9] They regulate a wide range of subjects: pastoral reorganization, ecumenism, ordained ministry, child protection, admission of the unconfirmed to Holy Communion, breakdown of pastoral relations, baptismal and marriage discipline, the ministry of readers, fees, the care and maintenance of property, the administration of liturgy, registers and records, and the quota system.[10] In the main quasi-legislation is addressed to clergy and lay office-holders, rarely to the laity generally, and its purpose is *supplementary*: to fill gaps in formal law; to clarify or interpret formal law; to provide for flexibility and pastoral sensitivity.

Sometimes the authorship, and therefore authority, of ecclesiastical quasi-legislation is easily identified: authority to make it is given expressly by synodical measure; sometimes it is created under an implicit discretion to do so; and sometimes authority to issue it is assumed, usually as a matter of 'good practice'. For example, the Incumbents (Vacation of Benefices) Measure 1977 (as amended 1993), places a *duty*, not a discretion, on the House of Bishops to formulate 'rules of guidance' to implement the Measure and 'to promulgate the rules of guidance in a Code of Practice'; it was

[9] For the lists of diocesan documents, see N. Doe, *The Legal Framework of the Church of England* (Oxford, 1996), pp.xv–xviii.

[10] See e.g. *Care of Churches and Ecclesiastical Jurisdiction Measure Code of Practice* (1993), provenance uncertain though probably the General Synod Office; *Good Practice in Group and Team Ministry* (1991); *Public Worship in the Church of England* (1986), issued 'by the authority of the Standing Committee of the General Synod'; *Liturgical Texts for Local Use: Guidelines and Copyright Information* (1988), provenance uncertain but probably the Liturgical Commission; *Anglican Marriage in England and Wales: A Guide to the Law for Clergy* (1992), Faculty Office of the Archbishop of Canterbury.

empowered 'at any time [to] amend or replace [the] Code of Practice', without a duty to lay the instrument before General Synod.[11] Occasionally *canons* confer a power to create instruments. The Clergy (Ordination) Measure 1990 enabled General Synod to empower by canon the provincial archbishop to grant a faculty allowing divorcees admission to Holy Orders. Canon C4(3A) provides that any application for a faculty by a diocesan bishop to the archbishop must be 'made and determined, in accordance with directions given from time to time by the Archbishops of Canterbury and York acting jointly'. The archbishops have since issued directions to regulate the procedure by which faculties are granted.

Sometimes the provenance of and authority to make quasi-legislation is less clear, particularly when parent legislation is silent. The Pastoral Measure 1983 *Code of Recommended Practice* was 'commissioned' 'by the Standing Committee of the General Synod under whose authority it is being published'; it is 'to serve as a standard reference document' concerning pastoral reorganization and associated matters, but 'Users must not regard the Code as a substitute for the Measure itself; paragraphs should always be read in conjunction with the sections of the measure to which they relate'. Indeed, the code recognizes that, further, 'the opportunity will be taken to issue leaflets or circulars on topics on which it is felt that additional guidance would be of help to practitioners'.[12] In the absence of express authorization by measure or canon, quasi-legislation may issue on the basis of an *assumed* rule-making authority,[13] though it may acquire an authority by adoption. In 1991 the Advisory Board of Ministry, 'on behalf of the House of Bishops', published *Regulations for Reader Ministry*; its introduction states: 'The House . . . accepted the Regulations . . . and authorised their publication for use in all dioceses.' They are 'intended to provide an agreed framework for further growth and development', seeking to 'clarify the basis of [readers'] duties and responsibilities and the practice of their ministry, and provide a

---

[11] Incumbents (Vacation of Benefices) Measure 1977, s.18.

[12] *Code of Recommended Practice*, pp.1, 5.

[13] *A Directory of Religious Life* (1990), issued by the Advisory Council on Relations of Bishops and Religious Communities: 'The Directory is . . . not a legislative code, but a corpus of norms or authoritative standards'; 'Adherence to these norms, like the acceptability of variations from them, is entrusted to the oversight of the Visitors of communities'.

common understanding *to be applied* in all dioceses'.[14] The authority underlying the Ecumenical Relations (Canons B43 and B44) *Code of Practice* is less easily identified. There is no indication on the face of the document as to provenance: it is simply 'published . . . by the General Synod of the Church of England'.[15]

The Language of Quasi-Legislation

Whilst general purposes of quasi-legislation are fairly easily recognized, often it is difficult to discover the immediate intention underlying the instrument and, therefore, whether the issuing body intends it to be binding on that body itself and on those to whom it is addressed. Intention is ascertained, needless to say, by the words. Both the language used and its clarity vary: sometimes imperative or prohibitive, sometimes permissive, exhortatory or aspirational, and sometimes ambiguous. The Salisbury *Diocesan Handbook* (1991) contains 'regulations' on selection and training of readers stating: 'The Bishop expects a *strict adherence* to the regulations both by the readers and by their incumbents.' Rochester's *Bishop's Guidelines* (1992) provide that 'Applicants for the position of pastoral assistant *must* have the backing and support of their Incumbents and PCC'. The *Chelmsford File* (1991) dealing with 'Extended Communion' provides that 'This practice is not authorised'. The same document prescribes that 'All incumbents and licensed ministers *are required* to take part in the Episcopal review programme'.

On the other hand, some provisions are normative. The Sheffield *Diocesan Handbook* (1994) provides that 'All clergy *should* take a day off each week (or two days each fortnight) and again parishes *should* help make this possible'. In the Priests (Ordination of Women) Measure 1993 *Code of Practice* the expression 'it would be *inappropriate* for' is commonly used.[16] Sometimes formulae are ambiguous. The Salisbury *Diocesan Handbook* (1991) prescribes that where a lay person other than a reader is asked to conduct a family service, 'written approval *should* first be sought from the

[14] ABM Policy Paper No. 2 (1991), p.1.
[15] See above, n.10.
[16] See e.g. para. 14.

Area Bishop', who, before giving permission, '*will* wish to satisfy himself', *inter alia*, that the person has received training.

Much quasi-legislation is not preceptive or prohibitive, but even permissive language is designed to regulate. The Church Commissioners' *Guide to Church of England Fees* (1986) is notable. Their Parochial Fees Order, secondary legislation under the Ecclesiastical Fees Measure 1986, prescribes that fees listed 'are to be payable to the persons named therein'. This does not impose a legal duty to demand the full fee but confers a discretion to *demand* a fee below the fixed maximum or to *waive* payment of any fee. Many diocesan regulations, based on the *Guide*, recognize a right of waiver if there is an acceptable pastoral reason; some dioceses, however, discourage the practice.

The Enforceability of Quasi-Legislation

On the one hand, the use of normative language suggests that quasi-legislation is not binding. On the other hand, the frequent use of mandatory terms generates the presumption that it is. Indeed, it cannot be said that no legal consequences flow from its creation or violation, either by its makers or its addressees. Two approaches to enforcement are possible: internal, within the church, and external, through judicial review by the secular courts. One problem is the absence of express consideration by ecclesiastical authorities, particularly church courts, of the status of extra-legal instruments.

First, quasi-legislation may have legal consequences for decision-making by the church courts. In *Re St James, Shirley* (1994) the Consistory Court gave effect to a 1992 'Response by the House of Bishops to Questions raised by the Diocesan Chancellors' concerning the position of fonts.[17] Similarly, guidelines issued by ecclesiastical judges may be said to have been enforced when applied in subsequent cases; they may bind when incorporated into the *ratio decidendi*.[18] Again, on several occasions since 1990 faculties

---

[17] [1994] Fam 134; this was the case 'even though the response was inconsistent with Canon F1(2)': M. Hill, *Ecclesiastical Law* (London, 1995), p.9.

[18] *Re Holy Innocents, Fallowfield* [1982] 3 WLR 666 at 667; *Re St Mary's, Banbury* [1987] 1 All ER 247 at 254; *Re St Luke the Evangelist, Maidstone* [1994] 3 WLR 1165.

have been refused when diocesan regulations had been violated.[19] Other forms of *dominium* regulation, such as Acts of Synod or of Convocation, according to orthodox learning, have only moral or persuasive force.[20]

Secondly, clerical disobedience of a prescriptive provision in quasi-legislation may be addressed by an executive episcopal direction and thereby might fall within the scope of canonical obedience. On one hand, if the provision were lawful, presumably episcopal directions based on it, being lawful, would have to be obeyed. Non-compliance might result, in an extreme case, in judicial proceedings for neglect of duty under the Ecclesiastical Jurisdiction Measure 1963. On the other hand, as was said in *Long v Bishop of Cape Town* (1863), 'the oath of canonical obedience does not mean that every clergyman will obey all the commands of the Bishop against which there is no law, but that he will obey all such commands as the Bishop by law is authorized to impose'.[21] In other words, only episcopal directions authorized by law – either by conferring a power to make them, or by being located in law which a bishop repeats – must be obeyed. With this argument, if law is silent, but quasi-legislation is not, the episcopal command is not 'lawful' and compliance is not required.

In secular government, quasi-legislation may have legal consequences in so far as it is considered by the courts in making decisions. The courts have three basic principles to determine whether quasi-legislation has legal force. First, the legitimacy test: if a line of authority to Parliament can be traced the courts are liable to give it greater weight or authority, particularly if it is published. Secondly, if the issuing body intended it to bind that body or its addressee, it will bind; intention to bind may be presumed from the language used, if for example it is expressed in clear and mandatory terms. Thirdly, it will bind if capable of enforcement.[22] The legality of all sorts of quasi-legislation has been determined by the secular courts – regulations, standing orders,

---

[19] *Re St Breoke, Wadebridge* [1990], *Ecclesiastical Law Journal*, 3 (1993), p.59; *Re St Chad's, Bishop's Tachbrook* [1991], ibid., p.60; *Re St Michael and All Angels, Thornhill* [1993], ibid. (1994), p.189; *Re Edward Charles Lee* (Deceased) [1995], ibid., 4 (1997), p.763.

[20] For a contrary view, see J. Burrows, 'Judicial Review and the Church of England', LL M dissertation, University of Wales, Cardiff, 1997.

[21] (1863) 1 Moo PCCNS 411 at 465.

[22] Baldwin and Houghton, 'Circular Arguments', p.239.

blanket resolutions, policy, directions, circulars, resolutions and guidance. Broadly, the courts may intervene if the body disregards or misconstrues rules of its own making. Indeed, publication may generate a 'legitimate expectation' that the rules will be properly and fairly applied – the courts will protect this expectation. Similarly, rules may be changed, but not arbitrarily to the prejudice of those who have reasonably relied upon them. A rule may be set aside by a court if it is found to be unreasonable, if it is manifestly unjust, oppressive or partial and unequal as between different classes.[23] There may also be a duty to follow 'guidance', but if guidance is erroneous in law it will have no legal force.[24]

The Legality of Quasi-Legislation

Borrowing from language employed to determine the validity of ecclesiastical custom: any ecclesiastical quasi-legislation *secundum legem*, declaratory of church law, or designed to implement it, will itself be lawful; quasi-legislation *praeter legem*, operating in the interstices of law, is lawful; quasi-legislation *contra legem* is unlawful. First, many instruments are declaratory of law or intended to implement it. The rule in the House of Bishops' *Regulations* that 'Readers are permitted . . . to read Morning and Evening Prayer (omitting the Absolution)' is declaratory of Canon E4(2)(b). The Sheffield *Diocesan Handbook* (1994) rule that 'All requests for lay persons, other than readers . . . to preach in parish churches at statutory services or otherwise *must* be referred direct to the Area Bishop for his express permission', is effectively a rearrangement of Canon B18(2).

Secondly, if law is silent on a subject this might generate a legal liberty to regulate that subject. Some quasi-legislation, however, is not easily identified as operating 'in addition' to law; sometimes it is unclear whether the provision is *against* law, or aims to restrict a

[23] For the relevant cases, see M. Fordham, *Judicial Review Handbook* (Chichester, 1995), p.52.

[24] *Laker Airways Ltd v Department of Trade* [1977] QB 643: although he accepted that 'the word "guidance" in section 3 of the Civil Aviation Act 1971 did not denote an order or command', Lord Denning concluded that 'while it is obliged to follow the [ministerial] guidance, the manner of doing so is for the [Civil Aviation] Authority itself'; Lawton LJ emphasized that 'guidance' and 'direction' were different: 'The word "guidance" has the implication of leading, pointing the way, whereas "direction" even today echoes its Latin root of *regere*, to rule.'

legal liberty. By Canon B22(5) a minister intending to baptize an infant whose parents reside outside the parish 'shall not proceed to the baptism *without having sought the goodwill* of the minister of the parish in which such parents reside' (unless the parent(s) is/are on the electoral roll). Here there is no duty to *obtain* the goodwill or consent of the other minister; nor is there a *right* in the other minister to veto the baptism. However, some diocesan regulations impose a duty to obtain the goodwill of the other minister; the Sheffield *Diocesan Handbook* (1994) prescribes 'The goodwill of the incumbent of the parish where they live should be obtained.'

Thirdly, quasi-legislation in conflict with church law, or state law, is illegal and of no force or effect, as when it seeks to restrict a legal liberty or fetter a discretion. By Canon B5 a minister may make minor, seemly and reverent liturgical variations not contrary to the doctrine of the church. The minister must decide these matters in the first instance but if there is any doubt a *right* exists to refer to the bishop: the matter 'may be referred'. If referred the bishop 'may give such pastoral guidance, advice or directions as he may think fit'. Whilst there is no canonical duty to refer, several diocesan regulations require that doubt about the 'definition' of such matters 'must be referred to the bishop'.[25] Again, under Canon B15A it seems that a baptized person who is confirmed or ready and desirous of being confirmed has a right to Holy Communion: 'There shall be admitted to the Holy Communion . . . members of the Church of England who have been confirmed . . . or are ready and desirous to be so confirmed'; there is no restriction that this right may only be exercised with prior episcopal approval. However, under House of Bishops' *Guidelines* (1997), ' "communion before confirmation" is a departure from our inherited norm, [and] requires special permission'; 'every diocesan bishop will have the discretion to make a general policy whether or not to entertain new applications for "communion before confirmation" to take place in his diocese'.[26]

[25] Rochester Bishop's *Guidelines* (1992), A.1; Wakefield, *Handbook of Information* (1989). ch.2, p.15.

[26] General Synod Misc 488; the Sacrament Act 1547 gives the right: the 'minister shall not without a lawful cause deny the same to any person that will devoutly and humbly desire it, any law, statute, ordinance or custom contrary thereto in any way notwithstanding'; see also: *R. v Dibdin* [1910] P 57; lawful cause is defined in Canon B16; nowhere, it would seem, does the law empower bishops to refuse admission to those in good standing who are ready and desirous to be confirmed.

Quasi-Legislation in the Anglican Communion

The Church of England is not alone in its employment of quasi-legislation. The phenomenon has begun to appear in many churches of the Anglican Communion. Guidelines are often made by national or provincial assemblies,[27] by the diocesan bishop,[28] or by administrative bodies,[29] dealing with a host of subjects, including doctrine and worship.[30] Sometimes church law prescribes that they must be considered by those to whom they are directed,[31] or that they should be observed,[32] that action must be 'in accordance' with them,[33] or that they must be followed,[34] and occasionally law requires clerical compliance with episcopal quasi-legislation.[35] However, recently it was held judicially that quasi-legislation of a central church assembly did not acquire binding force.[36] Unlike the Church of England some churches make an effort to define the authority of quasi-legislation as compared with

[27] See N. Doe, *Canon Law in the Anglican Communion* (Oxford, 1998), pp.21–3; e.g Protestant Episcopal Church in the USA, Canons, I.1.14(g): General Convention may make guidelines regarding the date and length of conventions.

[28] Protestant Episcopal Church in the USA, Canons, III.3.1: concerning lay ministers.

[29] Melanesia, Canons, E.5: the Salaries and Service Commission must issue guidelines to dioceses on clergy stipends and allowances.

[30] Papua New Guinea, Diocese of Port Moresby, Canon 10(3): 'The Bishop's guidelines will outline basic doctrine and procedures concerning the teaching of the faith and the administration of the sacraments. They will support the worship pattern, discipline and policies of the Provincial and Diocesan Constitutions, Canons and/or By-laws.'

[31] New Zealand, Canons, B.V.6: the parish must have 'proper regard' for guidelines issued by the Archives Committee.

[32] Scotland, Canon 52 and Resolution 9: diocesan synods 'should observe' guidelines on legislating.

[33] Philippines, Canons, 1.4.7: the Executive Council must seek missionaries 'in accordance with guidelines and criteria' determined by the Council.

[34] Papua New Guinea, Diocese of Port Moresby, Canon 10(3): 'All clergy . . . are subject to lawful obedience to the . . . Bishop's Guidelines'; New Zealand, Canons, G.VIII.1–3: General Synod may approve guidelines 'which shall be followed in administering the alternative practice' of admitting the unconfirmed to Holy Communion.

[35] Protestant Episcopal Church in the USA, Canons, IV.1.1: it is an ecclesiastical offence to violate episcopal 'Pastoral Directions'.

[36] *Stanton v Righter* (1996): the Court for the Trial of a Bishop, in the Anglican Church in the USA, decided that no doctrinal offence is committed when a bishop ordains a practising homosexual; 'the Church may forbid what has been done here, but not by a recommendatory resolution' of General Convention.

that of law properly so-called: law,[37] in the form of constitutions,[38] canons,[39] or acts,[40] is mandatory and binding; quasi-legislation is not, but is exhortatory in nature.[41]

Conclusions

The term ecclesiastical quasi-legislation is not simply an addition to an already bloated ecclesiastical legal vocabulary. Identifying informal rule-making as a normal function of ecclesiastical government confirms that church life cannot be regulated solely by formal, coercive law. Provincial and diocesan quasi-legislation is growing rapidly, and whilst this may mean less regulation by coercive law, it is symptomatic of a radical increase in ecclesiastical regulation generally. Whether it represents a new form of regulation by exhortation or persuasion is unclear, because of the language used and uncertainty over the applicability of principles being developed by the secular courts. The church seems to have followed the state, and in so doing, paradoxically, may be rediscovering the distinction between coercion and exhortation alluded to by Eric Kemp in 1957 – but the precise terms of this jurisprudential culture are far from clear.

[37] Australia, Canon 18, 1992: 'a law . . . shall be read as including a reference to a rule relating to discipline, a principle, a practice or a tradition of the Church of England'.

[38] Wales, Constitution, I.2: 'The Constitution shall be binding on all office-holders in the Church in Wales, all clerics and deaconesses . . . and all persons whose names are entered on the electoral roll of any parish.'

[39] Central Africa, Constitution, Definitions: 'By "Canon" is and shall be meant any measure passed by Synod which is intended to have a mandatory effect and to be part of the permanent corpus of Ecclesiastical Law of this Province.'

[40] Southern Africa, Standing Rules, 3(i): ' "Act" shall mean a regulation adopted by Synod which is intended to have a mandatory effect and to require any person . . . as of obligation, to perform or abstain from performing any action'.

[41] Ibid., 3(xiii): ' "Resolution" shall mean any expression of the judgement or opinion of the Synod, which is intended to have an appreciative, hortatory or advisory, and not a mandatory effect'.

10

Judicial Review
of Ecclesiastical Courts

MARK HILL

Recent years have seen a renaissance in the study of ecclesiastical law.[1] The contribution of Eric Kemp to such renaissance is well known. He has been an active and worthy president of the Ecclesiastical Law Society since its inception. Largely forgotten now[2] is the strict injunction issued by Henry VIII in October 1535 – and still presumably extant – forbidding the study of canon law in the universities.[3] Prurient media attention – in addition to legitimate academic interest – has attended the disciplining of errant clergy in the consistory courts. Not surprisingly these processes are presently the subject of a wholesale reconsideration by General Synod following the recommendations of the Hawker

---

[1] Note the formation of the Ecclesiastical Law Society in 1987, its increasing dialogue with the Canon Law Society of Great Britain and Ireland, the publication of the *Ecclesiastical Law Journal* and the degree of Master of Laws in Canon Law being taught at Cardiff Law School. See also M. Hill, *Ecclesiastical Law* (London, 1995), N. Doe, *The Legal Framework of the Church of England* (Oxford, 1996), and L. Leeder, *Ecclesiastical Law Handbook* (London, 1997).

[2] To the evident relief of Bishop Kemp and the author alike.

[3] When Thomas Cromwell was appointed Visitor of the University of Cambridge the King issued injunctions including, '5. That the study of canon law and degrees in it be abolished'. Thomas Leigh DCL of King's College was appointed to exercise the visitatorial powers. See D. R. Leader, *The History of the University of Cambridge,* vol.1, to 1546 (Cambridge, 1988), pp.332–3. For like provisions concerning the University of Oxford see P. Hughes, *The Reformation in England* (3rd edn. London, 1963), p.239. For a discussion as to the effectiveness of the prohibition, see R. H. Helmholz, *Roman Canon Law in Reformation England* (Cambridge, 1990), pp.152–3.

Report[4] which has itself been the subject of much comment.[5] The other main function of the consistory court, namely the exercise of the faculty jurisdiction[6] in relation to church buildings, their contents and their surroundings, is also under review.[7] This paper does not seek to address the merits or otherwise of the functioning of the consistory court in the discharge of its disciplinary or faculty jurisdiction. Instead it considers the related but thorny question of the extent to which the courts of the Church of England are amenable to the supervisory jurisdiction of the High Court by way of judicial review.[8]

As long ago as 1954 the Lloyd-Jacob Report[9] reviewed what it styled the 'jungle of courts' then existing in the Church of England and made certain recommendations. The writers of the report received evidence from, amongst others, the Reverend Canon E. W. Kemp (as he then was). The recommendations formed the basis of the present system of church courts which has its statutory origins in the Ecclesiastical Jurisdiction Measure 1963.[10] The supervisory role of the High Court of Justice was acknowledged in the report and is preserved in the Ecclesiastical Jurisdiction Measure itself.[11] The report commended that a statement of the right of any of Her

---

[4] *Under Authority*, The Report of the General Synod Working Party Reviewing Clergy Discipline and the Working of the Ecclesiastical Courts, GS 1217 (London, 1996).

[5] See, *inter alia*, *Ecclesiastical Law Journal*, 4 (1996), p.510 and 4 (1997), p.746.

[6] See generally G. H. and G. L. Newsom, *The Faculty Jurisdiction of the Church of England* (2nd edn. London, 1993) and Hill, *Ecclesiastical Law*, ch.7.

[7] See *A Review of the Ecclesiastical Exemption from Listed Building Controls*, conducted for the Department for Culture, Media and Sport and the Welsh Office by John Newman (September 1997).

[8] In preparing this paper I have been greatly assisted by J. Burrows, 'Judicial Review and the Church of England', LLM Dissertation, University of Wales, Cardiff, 1997. I am also grateful to Professor Sir David Williams QC and Dr Yvonne Cripps, both of Emmanuel College, Cambridge, for commenting on an earlier draft and, as always, to Dr Norman Doe and Fr Robert Ombres for their criticism.

[9] *The Ecclesiastical Courts: Principles of Reconstruction*, the Report of the Commission on Ecclesiastical Courts set up by the Archbishops of Canterbury and York in 1951 at the request of the Convocations (London, 1954). This expression appears at p.38.

[10] For a description of today's church courts see Hill, *Ecclesiastical Law*, ch.6.

[11] Lloyd-Jacob Report, *The Ecclesiastical Courts*, p.79; Ecclesiastical Jurisdiction Measure 1963, s.83(2): 'Nothing in this Measure affects . . . (c) any power of the High Court to control the proper exercise by ecclesiastical courts of their functions'.

Majesty's subjects who feels aggrieved for lack of justice or abuse of process in the proceedings of any ecclesiastical courts to apply at any stage in the proceedings to Her Majesty's High Court of Justice should find its place in any new set of canons. Thus the reconstructed courts would, it said, 'function subject to the safeguards provided by the common law to all Her Majesty's lieges whose liberty or property is in peril'. The report continued:

> Under this right every subject who complains of the proceedings of any domestic tribunal is entitled, either by prerogative writ issued from the Queen's Bench Division or by application for injunction in the Chancery Division, to have his case reviewed by the Supreme Court. If by transgression of its own rules or by disregard of the limits of its jurisdiction or the principles of natural justice, the domestic tribunal is shown to have fallen into error, the wrongful proceedings will be nullified.[12]

No such statement appeared in the canons of 1964 nor those of 1969. Today, in a climate of scandal and schism and in an increasingly secular and litigious society where wide-ranging reforms are heralded, it is timely to revisit the ecclesiastical courts and their amenability – or otherwise – to judicial review.

The traditional understanding of the supervisory role of the Divisional Court in relation to church courts relies upon the now outmoded distinction between the prerogative remedies of mandamus and prohibition on the one hand and writ of certiorari on the other.[13] As is well known, mandamus and prohibition regulate the extent of the jurisdiction of a court or tribunal by requiring it to act in cases which fall within its jurisdiction and preventing it from doing so in those which do not.[14] The writ of certiorari concerns the actual exercise of the jurisdiction. However, as is also well known, procedural reforms in 1977 replaced such distinct remedies with a new and comprehensive public law remedy

---

[12] Lloyd-Jacob Report, *The Ecclesiastical Courts*, p.79.

[13] See generally Halsbury, *Laws of England*, vol.14, *Ecclesiastical Law* (4th edn. London, 1975), paras. 301 and 1267–9.

[14] There is no doubt that in cases of this type judicial review lies. See *R. v North, ex parte Oakey* [1927] 1 KB 491; *Attorney-General v Dean and Chapter of Ripon Cathedral* [1945] Ch 239 and, by inference, *Attorney-General v British Broadcasting Corporation* [1981] AC 303 *per* Lord Edmund-Davies at 347A.

of judicial review.[15] The growth of this remedy over the past twenty years necessitates a rethinking of the received wisdom.

The 'traditional' analysis had been widely criticized even before the procedural reforms.[16] It relies heavily upon the judgment of the Court of Appeal in *R. v Chancellor of St Edmundsbury and Ipswich Diocese, ex parte White and Another.*[17] D. M. Gordon,[18] writing after the first-instance judgment,[19] but prior to the hearing of the appeal, questioned three broad propositions enunciated by the Divisional Court: that certiorari will never lie to an ecclesiastical court; that a court being subject to prohibition is not proof of its inferior rank; and that the ecclesiastical court is not an inferior court.

Gordon did not question that *ex parte White* was rightly decided.[20] He merely doubted the broader ramifications of those parts of the judgment which he considered to be strictly *obiter*. Certiorari, he reasoned, does run to an ecclesiastical court, had done so in the past, but would only rarely do so. There was a want of power in the High Court to examine any decision if it was removed from the ecclesiastical court. The latter exercised a wholly separate – though not foreign – body of canonical laws which the High Court was ill-equipped to determine. Accordingly the prerogative writ would prove futile. He concluded:

> It is quite conceivable that some future statute might well confer new judicial powers on an ecclesiastical court, powers not governed by ecclesiastical law, but to be exercised according to principles clearly defined in the Act. Then, it is submitted, a case might easily arise where a certiorari to quash would not be futile, would be the appropriate remedy, and ought to be granted; and so far as the language in [*ex parte White*] would bar the remedy, it is contrary to principle and authority.[21]

---

[15] S.I. 1977 No. 1955 and Order 53 of the Rules of the Supreme Court. See also the commentary at 53/1-14/1 of the Supreme Court Practice 1997; Newsom, and Newsom, *Faculty Jurisdiction*, p.7, and T. Briden and B. Hanson (eds.), *Moore's Introduction to English Canon Law* (3rd edn. London, 1992), p.111.

[16] See D. M. Gordon, 'Certiorari to an Ecclesiastical Court', *Law Quarterly Review*, 63 (1947), p.208.

[17] [1948] 1 KB 195 CA.

[18] See n.16.

[19] [1946] 2 All ER 604.

[20] *Ex hypothesi* it was rightly determined on appeal.

[21] Gordon, 'Certiorari', p.213.

For good or ill, the traditional analysis became the dogma of churchman and jurist alike. Recognition, however, must not be mistaken for approval. Sir William Wade QC has stated:

> Ecclesiastical courts are not subject to review by certiorari, since ecclesiastical law is a different system from the common law on which the ordinary courts will not sit in judgment. But prohibition will lie, not only to restrain the ecclesiastical court from exceeding its jurisdiction but also to prevent it from executing decisions marred by error of law, provided that the error is one which the court is competent to correct. Historical reasons lie behind this distinction. It is devoid of logic since if the court is prepared to assert control by prohibition it might as well do so by certiorari. Normally prohibition was only used in case of excess of jurisdiction, certiorari being the remedy for error of law. But in this context, having disclaimed the power to issue certiorari, the court extended the range of prohibition, thus remedying one anomaly by another.[22]

In a detailed critique of the functioning of the Church of England, Dr Norman Doe has sought to question the received wisdom, acknowledging the power of the High Court to issue mandamus[23] and, by implication, prohibition but describing the power to issue certiorari as, 'less clear'.[24] Commenting on *ex parte White* he indicates, as did Gordon, that the Court of Appeal merely held that the lack of a precedent to issue certiorari justified refusing the remedy and that: 'in the light of developments in judicial review in recent years, it might not be thought out of the question for certiorari to lie on evidence of a serious breach of the rules of natural justice, for example.'[25]

Such a result would not be entirely novel. In *R. v North, ex parte Oakey*[26] relief was granted to a vicar in the following circumstances. During restoration work for which a faculty had

---

[22] H. W. R. Wade and C. F. Forsyth, *Administrative Law* (7th edn. Oxford, 1994), pp.639-40.

[23] *R. v Archbishop of Canterbury* (1856) 6 E&B 546; *R v Arches Court Judge* (1857) 7 E&B 315; *R. v Bishop of London* (1889) 24 QBD 213 CA; *Allcroft v Lord Bishop of London, Lighton v Lord Bishop of London* [1891] AC 666 HL.

[24] Doe, *Legal Framework,* p.149.

[25] Ibid., p.150 n.122. See also Burrows, 'Judicial Review', ch. 3.

[26] [1927] 1 KB 491 CA.

been obtained a fresco was distempered over. Its obliteration was unauthorized by faculty but carried out with the knowledge of and without disapproval being expressed by the vicar. The painter's daughter, with the consent of the parochial church council, issued a petition for the restoration of the fresco alleging that its obliteration had occurred by order of the vicar. No relief against the vicar was claimed in the petition nor was he personally cited. On the hearing of the petition the faculty was granted and the vicar was ordered to pay the petitioner all expenses incurred in the restoration together with all her legal costs occasioned by the petition. The Divisional Court, by a majority, was of the opinion that the Chancellor had not exceeded his jurisdiction since the vicar, although technically not a party, had abundant notice of the proceedings and of the complaint being made against him. The Court of Appeal thought otherwise. Scrutton LJ stated:

> . . . to order a man to pay what is in the nature of a penalty for an offence without first giving him notice that an application for such an order is going to be made, is both contrary to the general law of the land, and is so vicious as to violate a fundamental principle of justice.[27]

Relief was granted, admittedly in the form of prohibition, even though arguably the vicar had a right of appeal to the Court of Arches. The contrary argument was that, not being a party, he had no such right. In any event, said Atkin LJ:

> I think it is quite plain that the fact of there being a remedy by way of appeal is no answer to a writ of prohibition, where the want of jurisdiction complained of is based upon *the breach of a fundamental principle of justice* such as I conceive to have been the case here.[28]

Further, recent developments in ecclesiastical law tend to suggest that in certain respects it is no longer such a separate system as to preclude the secular courts from adjudicating. Section 28(a) of the Ecclesiastical Jurisdiction Measure 1963 provided that the

[27] Ibid., p.504.
[28] Ibid., p.506 (emphasis added).

procedure at the trial of a priest in the consistory court should be the same as that of the court of assize exercising criminal jurisdiction. The crown court has now assumed the role of the court of assize. Though properly classified as an inferior court, it is exempt from judicial review.[29] No such express exemption exists in relation to the consistory court nor, curiously, are the various tribunals of the Church of England covered by the Tribunals and Inquiries Act 1992.[30] Equally, the 1963 Measure granted to the High Court power to inquire into contempts of the consistory court upon certification by the Chancellor.[31] On so doing, the High Court shall 'exercise the same jurisdiction and powers as if that person had been guilty of contempt of the High Court'.[32]

These factors, amongst others, render ecclesiastical law a less 'exotic system of law'[33] and more readily amenable to certiorari as heralded by Gordon.[34] When one considers the parallel evolution in the remedy of judicial review, the traditional analysis becomes still less tenable. A secular example of the practical distinction between certiorari and prohibition/mandamus is to be found in the role of the university visitor discussed at length in the speeches delivered in the House of Lords in *R. v Lord President of the Privy Council, ex parte Page*.[35] It was recognized that a university visitor had exclusive jurisdiction to determine what were the laws of the charity and their proper application. Lord Browne-Wilkinson observed that it extended,

> . . . so as to prohibit any subsequent review by the court of the correctness of a decision made by the visitor acting within his jurisdiction and *in accordance with the rules of natural justice*. This inability of the court to intervene is founded on the fact that the applicable law is not the common law of England but a peculiar or domestic law of which the visitor is the sole judge.[36]

---

[29] Supreme Court Act 1981, s.29(3).

[30] For a consideration of judicial review of quasi-judicial action in the Church of England see Doe, *Legal Framework*, pp.139–41.

[31] Ecclesiastical Jurisdiction Measure 1963, s.81(2).

[32] Ibid., s.81(3).

[33] To borrow from Gordon, 'Certiorari', p.208.

[34] It way well be that the 1963 Measure is the 'future statute' about which Gordon conjectured.

[35] [1993] AC 682 HL.

[36] Ibid., p.700E.

However, there is now (perhaps regrettably) very little which is exotic about the ecclesiastical law. Further, an analogy with the reasoning or result in *ex parte Page* would be difficult to sustain in the light of the comment of Lord Browne-Wilkinson that the visitatorial jurisdiction was, 'anomalous, indeed unique'.[37] Though cited by counsel in the course of argument in the House of Lords, no reference was made to *ex parte White* in any of the speeches delivered in *ex parte Page*, including the dissenting speech of Lord Slynn of Hadley in which Lord Mustill concurred.

Criticism of the traditional approach, however, has not been limited to academics. Judicial disquiet was voiced by the Divisional Court in *R. v Chancellor of the Chichester Consistory Court, ex parte News Group Newspapers Limited and Others*.[38] At the first trial of the Reverend T. M. Tyler,[39] the Chancellor excluded the press and public from the hearing of evidence. The charges against Mr Tyler raised issues of adultery and the Chancellor formed the view that the media were intent on reporting every salacious detail of the acts of sexual congress about which evidence was to be given. He noted that one or more of the witnesses had been in tears at the investigative stage of the proceedings. On application to the Divisional Court, Mann LJ referred to *ex parte White* and stated:

> In that case the Court of Appeal held that the writ of certiorari could not be issued to a consistory court and that that had been a long settled practice. The basis of the long settled practice seems to have been that although the Queen's Bench could intervene to prevent an exercise of jurisdiction or to prevent an excess of jurisdiction or to compel an exercise of jurisdiction, it could not intervene to correct errors committed within jurisdiction.[40]

However, although the *amicus curiae* indicated that the distinction between acts in excess of jurisdiction and acts within jurisdiction

---

[37] Ibid., p.704B.

[38] [1992] COD 48, Mann LJ and Hidden J. (CO/0175/91). The respondent ought properly to have been styled the Chancellor of the Diocese of Chichester but nothing turns on this error of appellation.

[39] The substantive appeal from the first trial is reported as *Burridge v Tyler* [1992] 1 All ER 437. A retrial was ordered at which it had been determined that evidence would be heard in public, hence the issue to be determined by the Divisional Court had become academic.

[40] Transcript pp.5H–6B.

was no longer sustainable,[41] Mann LJ concluded that, 'until the
Court of Appeal has an opportunity for reconsideration, the
distinction remains extant in relation to the ecclesiastical courts'.
He commented:

> The Court of Appeal might well now, if the occasion arises, decide that
> certiorari can go. If they do so decide, they may express the view that
> the courts should be cautious in exercising the review jurisdiction in
> regard to questions of ecclesiastical law because they are best left to the
> ecclesiastical courts with their own hierarchy of appeal.[42]

It is regrettable that the *amicus* did not seek to suggest that *ex
parte White* might have been decided *per incuriam* to the extent
that the salient part genuinely formed part of the *ratio*. It is
perhaps equally regrettable that the Divisional Court was not
disposed to take a more robust line itself. As it happened, it did not
need to do so since Mann LJ held that the court had jurisdiction to
entertain the newspaper's application: 'If I were asked to subsume
. . . exercise of jurisdiction under a now obsolete head, I would
subsume it under the head of intervention in regard to an act
alleged to be in excess of jurisdiction.'[43]

A more satisfactory and less elliptical resolution of the matter
might have been the assumption and exercise of principles of
judicial review *simpliciter*. To do so is not beyond the wit of the
judiciary. As was stated by the Master of the Rolls in *R. v The
Archbishops of Canterbury and York, ex parte Williamson*:

---

[41] Transcript at p.6D. Reliance was placed, unsurprisingly, on the speech of Lord
Diplock in *O'Reilly v Mackman* [1983] 2 AC 237 at 278D which itself cited Lord
Reid in *Anisminic Limited v Foreign Compensation Commission* [1969] 2 AC 147.

[42] Transcript at p.7B. This is consistent with the cautious approach adopted in
the exercise of judicial review of administrative acts by religious bodies. See Simon
Brown LJ at the application for leave in *R. v Ecclesiastical Committee of the
Houses of Parliament, ex parte Church Society* (1993) *Times*, 4 November citing
his earlier judgment in *R. v Chief Rabbi of the United Hebrew Congregations of
Great Britain and the Commonwealth, ex parte Wachmann* [1992] 1 WLR 1036 at
1042H.

[43] Transcript at p.7E. The matter under review was a decision of the Chancellor
to exclude press and public from a hearing in the consistory court pursuant to
s. 28(f) of the Ecclesiastical Jurisdiction Measure 1963. It was the opinion of the
Divisional Court that the Chancellor was wrong to proceed by reference to factors
such as the intimate nature of the allegations and analogies with statutory procedures. See Transcript 10G to 11G.

I hope it is unnecessary to say that the merits of this religious controversy [the ordination of women as priests] are a matter on which this court is not entitled to hold any opinion. Just as day by day the courts hear cases touching on political issues, and in doing so do their best to decide the legal questions before them without being drawn into any partisan position on those political issues, so here it is plainly the duty of the court to adjudicate on the legal questions raised in argument without taking up any position at all on the fundamental underlying issues.[44]

By way of postscript, both judicial review by order of certiorari and reconsideration by the Court of Appeal of *ex parte White* might be rendered otiose if the Human Rights Bill, which seeks to give domestic effect to the principles of the European Convention on Human Rights and which is presently before Parliament, is enacted as drafted.[45] Clause 6(1) will render it unlawful for a public authority to act in a way which is incompatible with one or more of the convention rights. Though vaguely defined, 'public authority' covers all bodies if the nature of their act is not private. This would include all Church of England ecclesiastical courts which would thenceforward be reviewable not merely for breaches of natural justice but arguably on theological and doctrinal issues as well. Eric Kemp, very much alive to the ramifications of the Human Rights Bill and doubtless mindful of *Re St Stephen's Walbrook*[46] where he delivered a lengthy judgment embracing doctrinal issues, has brought it to public attention.[47] The cautious approach in the

---

[44] (1994) *Times,* 9 March, *per* Sir Thomas Bingham MR. See transcript in Hill, *Ecclesiastical Law,* p.78. Equally, Simon Brown J. described judicial review as 'a dynamic area of law, well able to embrace new situations as justice requires'. See *R. v Jockey Club, ex parte RAM Racecourses Ltd* (1990) *Times,* 6 April.

[45] A detailed critique of the Bill may be found in G. Marshall, 'Patriating Rights – With Reservations: The Human Rights Bill 1998', in the University of Cambridge Centre for Public Law's *Constitutional Reform in the United Kingdom: Practice and Principles* (Oxford, 1998), pt.ii. See also J. M. Finnis, 'A Bill of Rights for Britain? The Moral of Contemporary Jurisprudence', Maccabaean Lecture (Oxford, 1985).

[46] [1987] Fam 146. Bishop Kemp's illuminating and erudite judgment as to what constitutes a holy table is forever preserved amongst decisions of judges of more conventional provenance, a treat for those with an affection for jurisprudential curios in the law reports.

[47] See a letter to *The Times* from Bishop Eric Kemp and Lord Lloyd of Berwick published on 6 March 1998.

review of essentially private church matters advocated by Mann LJ and others would be entirely abrogated.

The sooner the Court of Appeal looks again at *ex parte White* the better. There would now appear to be sufficient accreted justifications for judicial review to lie in respect of an ecclesiastical court acting in breach of natural justice as ventured by Doe and Burrows, as heralded by Gordon, as exemplified by *ex parte Oakey,* as sustainable under *ex parte Page* and as sought in *ex parte News Group*.[48]

---

[48] By way of addendum, as final page proofs were being processed, Chancellor Charles George QC drew to my attention the unreported judgment in *R. v Exeter Consistory Court, ex parte Cornish* (FC3 98–5690–4 24 June 1998), in which the Court of Appeal refused a renewed application for leave to move for judicial review of a decision of the Chancellor of the Diocese of Exeter. Waller LJ stated: 'In my judgment, we should look at this matter on its merits and not consider questions of jurisdiction.' The court did so and concluded that the applicant could not demonstrate that the Chancellor went wrong in law or reached an unreasonable result. I am encouraged by the approach adopted by the Court of Appeal but saddened that much of this paper may now be entirely redundant.

11

Religious Education
and Worship in State Schools

DAVID HARTE

Like 'law' itself, canon law can be an elusive concept to define. Historically, it certainly meant something very different from what it represents for English law at the end of the twentieth century.[1] However, it can be said that the canon-law tradition suggests an open-textured form of legislation which invites the modern, purposive, approach to interpretation and is particularly relevant for administrative law. The wide-ranging jurisdiction of the canon law in its heyday may embolden the modern lawyer who looks for a Christian dimension to today's law which goes well beyond the internal workings of the Church of England. The law relating to religion in state schools is a significant aspect of administrative law.[2] Because of its obvious importance for the Christian faith, it is a topic which is particularly appropriate to include in a review of the impact of canon law today.

This essay outlines how the present law preserves the opportunity for children in state schools in England to benefit from at least being introduced to the Christian faith, whilst safeguarding the position of families and teachers from other faiths and none. It discusses how these provisions may be seen in terms of canon or

---

[1] Cf. R. H. Helmholz, *Canon Law and the Law of England* (London and Rio Grande, 1987), and N. Doe, *The Legal Framework of the Church of England* (Oxford, 1996).

[2] J. D. C. Harte, 'Worship and Religious Education under the Education Reform Act 1988: A Lawyer's View', *British Journal of Religious Education*, 13 (1991), pp.152–61.

ecclesiastical law and their significance for the developing relationship between church and state.

The Religious Status of English State Schools

The modern system of national state education throughout England was created, as part of the welfare state, by the Education Act 1944. The system incorporated a large number of existing church schools, preserving their Christian ethos. Indeed, it was estimated that in 1944 half the schools in England were associated with the Church of England.[3] Most of these were classified as 'voluntary controlled schools' which were entirely dependent on state funding or as 'voluntary aided schools' which retained greater autonomy but were partly responsible for the upkeep of their buildings.[4] From the start, the voluntary sector was ecumenical, in that there was also a significant number of Roman Catholic church schools and a small group of Methodist and Jewish ones. The precedent has now been set for Muslim voluntary schools within the state sector. From 1944 ordinary local authority or 'county' schools were also required to provide both religious education and an act of worship to begin each day.[5]

Since 1944, the structure of state education has changed significantly. The original three strands of selective grammar schools and technical schools, with the majority of children relegated to secondary moderns, were superseded in most places by comprehensives.[6] However, the system remained the responsibility of local authorities. In the 1980s, the Conservative government introduced, as an alternative, new centrally funded, grant maintained schools[7] and city technology colleges.[8] The erosion of local control was increased in the 1990s with existing local authority schools being encouraged to manage their own budgets and to transfer to

---

[3] M. Cruikshank, *Church and State in English Education* (London, 1963), p.158.

[4] Now see Education Act 1996, ss.34 and 59-75.

[5] Now see Education Act 1996, Pt.V, Ch.III.

[6] The comprehensive system was introduced at a local level by administrative rather than statutory provisions; Circulars 10/65 and 10/66.

[7] Education Reform Act 1988, ss.52-104

[8] Ibid., s.105, see now Education Act 1996, ss.482–5.

centralized funding.[9] Nevertheless, grant maintained schools, like those of the local authorities, were required to provide religious education and worship. Elaborate provisions were made to retain the original ethos of schools which moved from local to central government control or to change it in accordance with parental wishes.[10]

The Labour government, elected in 1997, is reverting to a more locally controlled education system, but with considerable devolution of responsibility to all schools. The government has made clear its intention to safeguard the position of church schools and their distinctive ethos.[11] The nomenclature is being changed. However, existing church schools will be able to retain the relative autonomy of the old aided category, or, along with existing grant maintained schools, become foundation schools which will largely correspond to voluntary controlled schools.

By 1997, the proportion of church schools had shrunk considerably. Of over 7,500,000 children in the English state education system, only 1,500,000 were being taught, full time, in church schools.[12] Of 18,392 primary schools, 4,576 were attached to the Church of England, 1,773 to the Roman Catholic Church and 28 were Methodist. Of 3,569 secondary schools, only 199 belonged to the Church of England, although 359 were Roman Catholic.[13] Nevertheless, specifically Christian schools continue to form a significant part of the education system. The government elected in 1997 largely opposes selection of children on the basis of ability. However, it accepts that church schools may give priority to children whose parents genuinely desire a Christian ethos.[14] Equally significantly, the requirements for religious education and worship in ordinary state schools appear set to be retained. This is particularly striking in the case of worship, which there is considerable pressure from teachers' associations to abolish or to secularize.

---

[9] Education Act 1993.

[10] See at present Education Act 1996, ss.379-83.

[11] Department of Education and Employment, *Excellence in Schools*, 1997, Cm. 3681, p.67.

[12] Department of Education and Employment, *Statistics of Education: Schools in England 1997* (HMSO, London, 1998), p.21.

[13] Ibid., p.121.

[14] *Excellence in Schools*, p.71.

Religious Education in State Schools

Under the Education Act 1944, it was assumed that religious education and worship would be Christian, but it was provided that in non-church schools both should be non-denominational. The form taken by religious education was determined locally and the form of worship was largely left to individual headteachers. By 1988, general knowledge about Christianity in England had declined considerably, along with regular church-going. The Education Act 1988 introduced a new national curriculum. As originally planned, the Act would have ignored the position of religion. However, amendments brought about by effective lobbying from Christian pressure groups entrenched the requirement for schools to provide religious education and safeguarded the position of Christianity in syllabuses, whilst providing more effectively for the syllabuses to be determined locally by education authority conferences. Each conference includes groups representing faiths other than the established church, the Church of England, teachers and the local authority. A majority of each group is required to approve a syllabus and each syllabus must be reviewed every five years.[15]

Agreed syllabuses for religious education are used in county schools, or as they will be known in future, community schools.[16] In each local authority area, the agreed syllabus is also followed in grant maintained schools which do not have a specific faith foundation.[17] The same arrangements appear set to continue where these grant maintained schools are changed to the new category of foundation schools. For each local authority, a Standing Advisory Committee on Religious Education (SACRE), similarly composed to the initial syllabus conference, continues to monitor the religious education and also worship which is provided in individual schools.[18]

A striking requirement of the 1988 Act was that agreed syllabuses should 'reflect the fact that the religious traditions in Britain are in the main Christian whilst taking account of the teaching and practices of other principal religions represented in Great Britain'.[19]

---

[15] Education Act 1996, s.375 and Sch.31.
[16] Ibid., s.376.
[17] Ibid., ss.379–383.
[18] Ibid., ss.390–1.
[19] Education Reform Act 1988, s.8; now Education Act 1996, s.375(3).

It is unusual to find a rule stating its own premises in such a manner, as a simple matter of fact. The provision is also interesting because of its very open-ended character. In common with much of modern statutory administrative law, it specifies factors which are to be taken into account in decision-making but leaves a large measure of discretion to the decision-makers in how those factors are to be weighed. It is clear that agreed syllabuses must at least have a substantial Christian content and must give some room for the treatment of other major religions such as Islam and Hinduism. However, the quantity of Christian content and the form it should take is not prescribed. It may be considered a striking omission that there is no requirement that children should actually read the Bible.

It is difficult for concerned parents to challenge an agreed syllabus in the courts. In the case of *R and D*,[20] two mothers complained that religious education was inadequately provided in the integrated curriculum run by a primary school, but the judge, McCullough J., simply declined to consider this aspect of the case on the basis that the children concerned had already been moved to another school.

There are strong differences of opinion, not least within the Church of England, over the form which agreed syllabuses should take and how explicitly Christian they should be.[21] However, the 1988 Act made clear that the intention was to provide a foundation of knowledge and understanding which would enable pupils to respect the faith of others, whilst allowing them the opportunity to make their own commitment if they chose so to do. Thus, the Act referred to 'religious education', rather than 'religious instruction', the term used in 1944. On the other hand, a rather prickly restriction in the 1944 Act banning teaching in non-denominational schools by means of 'catechisms or formularies',[22] was modified to

---

[20] *R. v Secretary of State for Education, ex parte R and D*, unreported, CO/2209/92, 26 February 1993, commented on by A. Bradney, 'Christian Worship?', *Education and Law*, 8 (1996), p.127.

[21] The topic is a recurring theme in the *British Journal of Religious Education*. See e.g. Shaik Abdul Mahbud, 'A Muslim Response to the Education Reform Act 1988', *British Journal of Religious Education*, 14 (1992), p.88; G. Robinson, 'Religious Education, Government Policy and Professional Practice, 1985–1995', *British Journal of Religious Education*, 19 (1996), p.13; cf. J. Burn and C. Hart, *The Crisis in Religious Education* (Newcastle, 1988); C. Hart, 'Legislation and Religious Education', *Education and the Law*, 5 (1993), p.7.

[22] Education Act 1944, s.26(2).

make clear that these could be studied, although, by implication, not merely learnt unquestioningly by rote.[23]

Church of England schools are free to follow their own syllabuses.[24] However, in the case of voluntary controlled schools this has required initiatives to be taken by concerned parents.[25] In practice, syllabuses for church schools are normally prepared by dioceses. Like agreed local authority syllabuses, some produced by dioceses have been criticized as syncretistic and lacking sufficient Christian content.[26] There are no statutory requirements as to content which parents could rely on to challenge the adequacy of a diocesan syllabus. On one view, this suggests that the church has less concern for individual rights than does the secular law. On another view, it would be inappropriate for statute to provide an opportunity for doctrinal matters to be raised as an issue in the secular courts.

Worship in State Schools

In county schools, the Education Reform Act 1988 provided that the daily worship which had been required since 1944 must be 'wholly or mainly of a broadly Christian character'.[27] To make this feasible the requirement of an act of worship at the beginning of the school day was relaxed to allow assemblies to be in smaller groups and at different times.[28] However, the requirement for worship is now more explicitly Christian than that for religious education. The subject of school worship has proved correspondingly more contentious, despite the freedom of both parents[29] and teachers[30] to opt out. Most strikingly, the legislation allows a SACRE to disapply the requirement in any county school, or for a particular class or description of pupils, that daily worship should have an essentially Christian character.[31] The SACRE has a very

[23] Education Reform Act 1988, s.9(10) and Sch.1, para.1; now Education Act 1996, s.376(2).
[24] Education Act 1996, ss.377 and 378.
[25] Ibid., s.377.
[26] E.g. compare the more traditional syllabus for the Diocese of Chester with the multi-faith emphasis of the Manchester syllabus.
[27] Education Reform Act 1988, s.7; now Education Act 1996, s.386(2).
[28] Education Reform Act 1988, s.6(2); now Education Act 1996, s.385(2).
[29] Education Act 1996, s.389.
[30] Ibid., s.146.
[31] Ibid., s.387.

wide-ranging discretion and merely needs to determine that the explicit requirement as to Christianity 'is not appropriate'. In making the determination it is to 'have regard to any circumstances relating to the family backgrounds of the pupils'.[32] The initiative for such a determination is taken by the headteacher through the local education authority, following consultation with parents and governors. It is revealing of the apparently secular ethos of much of the teaching profession today, that, rather than relying on these exceptions, its leaders have argued for the abolition of the basic requirement of worship altogether.

By contrast, arrangements for worship have been challenged for lacking Christian content, by parents who are concerned to preserve worship as part of the normal school experience. In R and D,[33] McCullough J. rejected criticism of the worship in a Manchester primary school which parents had argued was insufficiently Christian. The judge agreed with the approach of the Secretary of State for Education that worship[34] 'must in some sense reflect something special or separate from ordinary school activities. [It] should be concerned with reverence or veneration paid to a being or power regarded as supernatural or divine and . . . the pupil, at his or her level, should be capable of perceiving this'. However, as far as the Christian element was concerned the judge was vague. It was sufficient that the person of Jesus should be recognized as having a 'special status'. The judge stressed the importance of providing worship which was accessible to children from a non-Christian background, rather than its function in informing the faith of children from a Christian background. Thus, the worship should be consistent with Christian belief but should avoid conflicting with other beliefs held in the community.

The pattern of worship in non-church schools depends very much, therefore, on a positive approach from all concerned. There is scope for a body of Christian parents and teachers to ensure genuinely prayerful Christian assemblies. An interfaith approach may provide worship in the forms of a variety of faiths, giving a dominant role to Christianity. Curiously, it is not permissible to provide worship in a form distinctive of any particular Christian or

[32] Ibid., s.394(2).
[33] See n.20.
[34] Department of Education, Circular 3/89.

other denomination.[35] This bar on traditional forms of worship seems redolent of an outdated suspicion between denominations. It also suggests that all those present will join in the act of worship.

A more realistic and effective method may be for individuals from a particular tradition to offer worship in front of an assembly, so that pupils may learn to appreciate and respect differences. There is scope within the wording of the legislation for creative development of new patterns of worship in school assemblies which would affirm what those present may be expected to have in common, whilst avoiding a syncretistic mixture of conflicting elements. The requirement of 'collective worship of a broadly Christian character' is revealing in that it recognizes Christianity as the established religion of the nation whilst distancing the Church of England as one of a number of denominations.

Many ecumenical initiatives have foundered through the fear of losing cherished and distinctive features of existing denominations. By contrast, enduring local initiatives have been made in sharing church buildings and regular worship. These initiatives have been made possible by suitable legal instruments.[36] It is particularly significant that a building licensed by the bishop as the centre of worship for a parish may serve equally as a local Methodist or United Reformed Church. A single congregation may transcend denominational divisions and so serve to bind together the wider denominations concerned. The pattern of shared worship for such a congregation may involve separate but shared services using the different liturgies of the constituent traditions or it may develop as a distinctive liturgy in itself. The legal framework for worship in schools suggests the second approach. The ban on the traditions of a particular denomination may restrict some liturgical forms of worship. However, it may be an advantage that there is no obligation to provide a particular service, as there would be in a parish church. This may allow the opportunity for developing new forms of worship for local schools which are truly ecumenical.[37]

Meetings between Christians from different churches could take on a new momentum if they focused on praying for and developing

---

[35] Ibid., ss.386(3) and 387(2).

[36] Sharing of Church Buildings Act 1969.

[37] For some practical considerations see D. W. Lankshear, *Churches Serving Schools* (London, 1996).

forms of prayer and collections of readings for the local community school. This new name for county schools is intended to emphasize the central place of the school in the local community. The opportunity to develop new and relevant patterns of worship in community schools will last only so long as religion, and indeed the Christian religion, is still legally afforded a place in the ordinary state curriculum. If the opportunity is not taken and worship in schools disappears by default, through pressures on the timetable and the indifference of teachers and parents, this could prove to be a major charge on the indictment for disunity against the church.

The Character of the Legal Framework for Religion in Schools

The distinctive legal provisions for religious education and worship in English schools are largely a matter of secular law, which the churches and individual Christians in Parliament have played a significant role in shaping. However, the framework for voluntary Church of England schools is a part of the ecclesiastical law regulating an aspect of the Church. It is therefore perhaps surprising that the Church seems to play little part in legislating for these schools through the General Synod. Education may feature from time to time in debates in the Synod and syllabuses for religious education in Church of England schools are devised at a diocesan level. However, church schools are not the subject of canons, nor to any large extent of Measures emanating from the Synod or its predecessor, the Church Assembly.[38]

There is scope for concerned parents and other Christians to challenge inadequacies in both religious education and worship in state schools, whether denominational or not, by seeking judicial review.[39] Where secular law sets out a general framework for religious education and worship, striking the right balance will be largely a matter of administrative discretion for local education

---

[38] Clergy may be licensed to perform offices and services at a school in a different parish; Extra Parochial Ministry Measure 1967, s.2. Power is given by Measure for the Church Commissioners to support church aided schools financially: Church Schools (Assistance by Church Commissioners) Measure 1958.

[39] R. v Secretary of State for Education, ex parte R and D, unreported, CO/2209/92.

authorities, governors and headteachers. On the other hand, on normal principles of administrative law, policies which blatantly and unreasonably go outside the statutory principles could be the subject of review. For example, a local authority agreed syllabus might be challenged if it confined the time to be allocated to Christianity for any pupil in any year to less than 50 per cent of hours spent on religious education. A school could be challenged if it provided for a regular act of worship which was inconsistent with orthodox Christian belief. Well targeted court cases may help to refine relevant principles and the limits of what is permissible.[40]

The idea of liberty in English law assumes that the citizen is free to do what he or she wishes unless they interfere with the rights of others or break a specific public law requirement, normally by committing a criminal offence. However, the reality is that the ordinary citizen has little scope for freedom of expression without financial resources or specific statutory rights. The concept of a general liberty carries little weight where, for example, parents are pitted against the state in seeking a suitable education for their children. It is therefore crucial that education law should provide specific rights for children to be educated in accordance with the wishes of their parents[41] and for parents to be able to withdraw children from education which is unacceptable. Such rights of withdrawal are provided in respect of both religious education and worship.[42] A similar right to withdraw applies to sex education.[43] This is significant, since sex education is an area of potential conflict with Christian morality. The civil liberties, rights based approach is set to become increasingly prominent in English law with the incorporation of the European Convention on Human Rights, a subject which is beyond the bounds of this essay.[44]

The common law depends upon a potential litigant identifying a point of dispute and claiming a remedy. Common law judges are traditionally reluctant to make statements of principle except in the context of an express dispute. In the world this may be a realistic attitude. A dispute sharpens the legal character of the

[40] Harte, 'Worship and Religious Education'.
[41] Education Act 1996, s.9.
[42] Ibid., s.389.
[43] Ibid., s.405.
[44] Cf. J. Rivers, 'Does the UK Need a Bill of Human Rights?', in P. Beaumont (ed.), Christian Perspectives on Law Reform (Carlisle, 1998).

issue and arguing over academic points can be a waste of valuable court time. However, if clarifying the law is dependent upon disputes, individual litigants bear a heavy burden in monetary costs and anxiety in discovering underlying principles to benefit the public. The modern emphasis on human rights is calculated to encourage litigation. This may help to clarify the law but it adds to the stresses of modern society.

Where the law is unclear, particularly where it lays down broad rules which need to be developed in practice, litigation may, therefore, be valuable for identifying underlying principles and in clarifying how they should be applied consistently. However, it will be less costly of money and of good relationships if principles can be identified, agreed and clearly expressed without the need for litigation. There is often a suspicion of law in church quarters, partly because of a theological emphasis on grace, to the disadvantage of law, and partly for fear of litigation. However, the best way to avoid disputes is not to shun the law, so much as to concentrate on improving its quality. There is, therefore, much scope for a contribution by Christian lawyers to improve the framework for religious education in all schools.

The development of theologically sound principles in a clear and readily applicable form, in areas such as education law, is a real challenge for canon lawyers. In framing legislation, the canon-law tradition may suggest a basis for offering clear guidance so as to regulate behaviour, whilst avoiding the self-centred approach of rights based law. Some concept of an advisory decree may offer an authoritative alternative, here, to the judgment arising from a disputed case. It is noteworthy that advisory opinions on matters of church law are sought by the General Synod from a formally constituted Legal Advisory Commission and are published for the general benefit of the Church and others. A similar approach may be identified in the advice given by secular circulars from government departments. Perhaps papal decrees in early canon law could be said to provide a precedent.

Religion in Schools and the Future Relationship between Church and State

In a society which is generally pluralist, particularly in religious terms, tensions are inevitable and the law is required to provide a framework within which those tensions may at least be contained. It is a function of the law to direct tensions constructively, so as to promote greater mutual respect and to deepen understanding of the fundamental faith of each individual and community. In the English state school system, this may mean reassessing the orientation of individual schools. The recent incorporation of Muslim voluntary schools has been welcomed by church representatives. If these schools are a success, further applications may be expected in areas with large Asian populations. However, it should be of equal concern for Christian families to ensure adequate opportunities for their children to be nurtured in a Christian environment. Often Christian parents of any denomination will be happy with the ethos of a community school. In other cases, however, the machinery which is available could be used more effectively to establish new church schools.

The Church of England prides itself, as a national church, in serving the nation locally, through the parish system. Many of the existing Church of England voluntary schools will have begun as parish schools. However, even at primary level, there are areas where they are thin on the ground. In a new housing scheme, for example, there may be a new parish church or ecumenical centre, but no church school. It is surprising that there is no national church policy to ensure that every family has ready access to a Christian primary school. In areas where there are no church primary schools but where there are community schools with a Christian ethos it would be easier to preserve that ethos if it were possible to appoint reserved teachers in community schools to teach the Christian religion, where that is desired by parents.

At the secondary stage, there are relatively few church schools, partly because of the amalgamation of smaller institutions. It is at this age that children from Christian backgrounds are often alien- ated from their parents' faith but also when any child may be open to the challenge of a mature and intellectually coherent explanation of the faith. There are immense opportunities for partnership by the church with schools, sharing teaching facilities for young people with continuing education programmes at parish or deanery level. The use of the Internet and of broadcasting offer the possibility of increasingly high-quality Christian materials which are economically feasible to use. If the choral tradition which clings on in cathedrals were revived in parishes it could help to meet the call to restore and expand music as part of the ordinary school curriculum.

It is part of the Christian heritage of England that faith is largely free to permeate every aspect of life. It is not excluded from the classroom or the staff common room, as it would be in countries such as the United States of America, or, even more, France. The experience of the Church of England in accommodating the demands of Dissenting traditions since the eighteenth century made possible a generally Christian perspective in the Education Act 1944. The fact that that the religious content of the 1944 Act was implicitly, rather than explicitly Christian, led to tensions in making provision within the system for growing communities from other faiths. However, both the earlier experience with Dissent and the unspecific wording of the obligations to provide religious education and worship in the 1944 Act provided the basis for a new settlement in the Education Reform Act 1988. This settlement recognizes the aspirations and value of other faith communities, whilst reaffirming the central Christian traditions of the nation. It is a settlement, cast in legal terms, not for a secular society but for one which is genuinely pluralist.

12

Establishment
in a European Context

DAVID McCLEAN

Those who regularly set examination questions will be familiar with the (distinctly unfriendly) technique of inviting discussion of a topic in deliberately inappropriate terms. As with such questions, so with the title of this essay. An awareness of the patterns of church–state relations in other European countries is, however, an important background to the English debate, and may serve to improve the focus and quality of that debate.

The reference in the title of this essay to a European context may raise hopes, or fears, that the further development of European institutions may bring about not just a common internal market and a common currency but also a 'European' understanding of the role of the church in its relationship to the secular political authorities. Use of the word 'establishment' highlights, however, the intimate relationship between the church – or particular churches – and individual nation-states. That relationship is expressed in markedly different ways,[1] an unsurprising result of geography, history (both ecclesiastical and secular), and of the cultural diversity of the countries of Europe.

As a result of pressure from the churches, in which the German churches (both the *Evangelische Kirche in Deutschland* and the German Catholic Bishops' Conference) took a leading role, the

---

[1] For a full comparative examination, see the European Consortium for Church–State Research's volume on *The Constitutional Status of Churches in European Union States* (Milan, 1995); and G. Robbers (ed.), *Church and State in the European Union* (Baden-Baden, 1996: published in five languages).

Inter-Governmental Conference which produced the Treaty of Amsterdam 1997 included a Declaration on the Churches in its Final Act. This reads in part: 'The European Union respects and does not prejudice the status under national law of churches and religious associations or communities in the Member States.' This not only provides an express reference to the churches and religious considerations in the corpus of European Union texts, which previously had largely lacked that dimension, but also ensures that the constitutional position of the churches remains a matter for the national law of each member state.

Partly for that reason, we might be wise in a discussion of the position in European countries to shun that blessed word 'establishment'. It carries too many associations which are peculiarly British.[2] European debate uses a variety of terms, of which the German *Staatskirchenrecht*, state and churches law, is perhaps one of the more exact, though we need to recall that the issues are not necessarily of exclusive concern to the Christian churches but must take account not only of the long-established Jewish presence but also the growing significance of Islam in Europe.

The Continuing Importance of the Issue

It is a striking fact that in every European country the issue of church–state relations is of present-day interest. No state regards 'religion' as a private matter of such little importance that, like some leisure activity, it can be passed over in silence in the statute book. Indeed articles on the church are to be found in almost every written constitution (even if only to proclaim a regime of separation), and every state is a party to the European Convention on Human Rights with its Article 9 on the Freedom of Religion.[3] So it is that even an avowedly secular state finds itself recognizing the

---

[2] Though of course it means different things in England and Scotland, just as 'disestablishment' means rather different things to the Church of Ireland and the Church in Wales. See T. G. Watkin, 'Vestiges of Establishment: The Ecclesiastical and Canon Law of the Church in Wales', *Ecclesiastical Law Journal*, 2 (1990), p.110.

[3] Article 9(1) reads 'Everyone has the right to freedom of thought, conscience and religion; this right includes freedom to change his religion or belief and freedom, either alone or in community with others and in public or private, to manifest his religion or belief, in worship, teaching, practice and observance.'

importance of religious belief in its fundamental legal texts. Nowhere is this better illustrated than in Article 2 of the Constitution of the Fifth French Republic of 1958, which includes the following: 'France is a Republic which is indivisible, secular (*laïque*), democratic and social. It guarantees equality before the law to all its citizens, without distinction of origin, race or religion. It respects all forms of belief.'[4] As will appear below, the *laïcité* of the French Republic is an oddly compromised one.

European analysis therefore tends to begin with the freedom of religion, and its constitutional guarantees. Given that such a freedom must involve association with other believers, the next question is whether and to what extent that gives a special status to the churches as such, and how any such status is expressed.

A Privileged Position

One approach gives a privileged relationship with the state, an intimacy, a special place at the heart of the nation's institutions, perhaps involving the legislature or, more often, the head of state. For example, Article 33 of the Greek Constitution requires the president of the Republic to take an oath invoking the Holy Consubstantial and Indivisible Trinity. The Danish Constitution of 1953, having declared[5] that 'the Evangelical-Lutheran Church is the Danish national church and as such is supported by the State', requires the sovereign to belong to that church,[6] just as the queen of England must 'join in communion with' the Church of England.[7]

The privileged relationship may not confer only benefits on the church. As Hoffman J. pointed out with great clarity in 1994, 'A religion may be established or unestablished. The essential distinction is that an established religion is subject to state control as regards doctrine, government and discipline, but an unestablished religion . . . is not.'[8] In Denmark the association of church and state is very

---

[4] 'La France est une République indivisible, laïque, démocratique et sociale. Elle assure l'égalité devant la loi de tous les citoyens sans distinction d'origine, de race ou de religion. Elle respecte toutes les croyances.'

[5] Art.4.

[6] Art.6.

[7] Act of Settlement 1700, s.3.

[8] *Williamson v The Archbishops of Canterbury and York* (Chancery Division, 11 November 1994).

close, with a minister for Ecclesiastical Affairs having wide responsibilities for the national church. As is well known, this seriously handicapped that church in dealing with ecumenical initiatives, especially those with an international dimension, until some freedom of manœuvre was given in the 1989 Act on Participation by the National Church in Ecclesiastical Work.

Even more striking is the degree of control exercised by the state over appointments in 'privileged' churches. Although in practice the state's involvement is generally formal and instances of active intervention by political leaders are rare and controversial,[9] some measure of state control is found in Denmark, England, Finland, and in some of the Swiss cantons, and the president of the French Republic has a role in Alsace-Moselle.

A Position of Autonomy

The alternative approach is to allow the church a privilege of a different sort, a privileged freedom from state interference. However all-embracing the legislative power of the state may be in principle, the church is allowed a 'space' of its own which the state does not invade. This is not the result of mere lack of interest, but of a positive legal (often constitutional) provision as to autonomy.

An example is to be found in the German position. Article 140 of the Constitution, by incorporating articles from the Weimar Constitution of 11 August 1919, ensures that the state is not allowed to take decisive action in the affairs of religious communities.[10] Article 137(3) of the Weimar text provides that 'Every religious community regulates and administers its own affairs independently within the framework of the laws that are valid for all.' The Belgian Constitution of 1994 has a very specific provision: 'The State has no right to interfere in the nomination or installation of ministers of religion, nor to prevent them communicating with their superiors or from engaging in publishing, subject in this last case to the general laws as to the press and publishing.'[11] Doctrinal writings have

---

[9] As in the case of the appointment of the bishop of Basle in 1994 and of a bishop of Liverpool in 1997.

[10] This German usage refers to churches and similar religious groups, not to 'religious communities' in the sense of religious orders of monks or nuns.

[11] Art.21.

elaborated the notion of autonomy, and there is a growing body of case-law on the extent to which internal church decisions are exempt from normal processes of judicial review.[12]

While the privileged position described above is likely to be enjoyed by a single national or established church, autonomy may be granted more widely. So Austria has a provision dating from 1867 that 'every *legally recognised* church or religious community . . . orders and manages independently its internal affairs',[13] and there are elaborate procedures for the designation of such recognized churches.[14]

The Special Case of Church Legislation

In a number of states, including the United Kingdom, primary legislation on church matters is handled in a special way. As with the more general issues already noted, this can be seen as a privilege or a burden. The argument can become quite complex. For example, some of the supporters of controversial legislation concerning the Church of England, such as the women priests legislation, were unhappy that after being passed by the General Synod by two-thirds majorities in each House of Synod it still had to run the gamut of the Ecclesiastical Committee and be debated in each House of Parliament. On the other hand, the issue was placed on the parliamentary agenda by the decision of the Synod; had the decision been one for secular politicians the issue might have been post-poned, or tackled earlier, as the government of the day perceived political advantage in so deciding. Of course were ecclesiastical law to cease to exist as law, as in Wales after the disestablishment of the Church in Wales, the issue would not arise in that form, although the religious exemption to the sex discrimination legislation would remain an issue.

It is less well known that Finland has a procedure for the consideration of ecclesiastical legislation remarkably like that in England.

[12] See R. Torfs, 'La Régime constitutionel des cultes en Belgique', in the European Consortium volume referred to above, n.1.

[13] Emphasis added. Staatsgrundgesetz über die allgemeinen Rechte der Staatsbürger, Art.15.

[14] See R. Potz, '*Suum Cuique:* The Parity of Recognised Churches and Religious Communities in Austria', *European Journal for Church and State Research (EJCSR),* 4 (1997), p.187.

Section 83 of the Constitution of 1919 provided for a Church Code which contains provisions on the organization and administration of the Evangelical Lutheran Church. Special provisions apply to amendments to the code which are proposed solely on the initiative of the Church, are approved by the General Synod of the Evangelical Lutheran Church, and introduced into Parliament by the government; Parliament can approve or disapprove but not amend the Bill. This special procedure has been criticized by the commission preparing a new constitution for adoption in the year 2000. It proposed the removal of the ban on parliamentary amendment of Synod proposals, with the safeguard that the Bill would not be enacted unless the Church was content with the text as finally settled by Parliament. In 1996 the Church Council, in response to a request by the Minister of Justice, refused to endorse these proposals, but indicated that it would not object to Parliament being allowed to make technical, as opposed to substantive, amendments to Church Bills.[15]

It would, however, be a mistake to concentrate overmuch on constitutional issues of this type. One of the characteristics of the discussion of establishment in England is that it all too often focuses on a narrow range of issues, principally the more picturesque aspects of our unwritten constitution: the Sovereign as Supreme Governor and as Defender of the Faith; the presence in Parliament of the Lords Spiritual. Quite apart from the pastoral and spiritual responsibilities and opportunities which are the lot of any 'national' or 'majority' church, whatever its constitutional position, some very practical links between church and state need to be explored and weighed.

The Legal Quality of the Churches

At first sight, this may seem very much a matter of 'lawyers' law', but it can have significant practical effects. How, in purely legal terms, do we classify a church as an entity? It is an association of individuals, organized for specific purposes; the nature of the association, and the nature of those purposes, have no exact parallels. So how do we place a church in relation to the various

[15] See J. Seppo, 'Church and State in Finland 1996', *EJCSR*, 4 (1997), p.149 at pp.152–3.

types of entity (corporations, business associations, voluntary societies, charitable trusts) known to particular legal systems? On what terms (if at all) does a church own its buildings? How does it stand in relation to employment law so far as its clergy or ministers are concerned?

For example, in German law the major churches have the status of 'public law corporations', a status granted where the church in question satisfies criteria as to the length of its existence and the size of its membership.[16] In Switzerland, churches enjoy public law status in most, but not all, cantons; but the attributes of that status vary widely from canton to canton.[17] In Austria, some churches have the status of public corporations, though with rather different attributes than other corporations under public law; and it seems very difficult for other churches to acquire any sort of legal personality whether under public or private law.[18]

The closer the link between a church and the state, the less likely it is to enjoy separate legal personality. The Church of England, for example, is not a legal entity capable of owning property, or of suing or being sued. The same is true of the churches of Denmark and of Sweden; the current proposals for a loosening of the bonds between church and state make the latter a particularly interesting case. Under the proposals, a new and specific type of legal entity, the 'registered religious community', would be created, with a large measure of internal autonomy such that parliamentary legislation designed to affect them would have to be passed by two successive Parliaments. The Church of Sweden would enjoy the new status under a special Act; other churches would gain it by approved registration.[19]

Such a special legal status has certain clear advantages. It recognizes the distinctive nature of a church, in a way which other legal devices do not. For example, the use in England of the trust as a device for holding the property of non-Anglican churches, and indeed the use of corporate Boards of Finance in Anglican dioceses, does not accurately reflect the churches' own understanding of their structures.

---

[16] Art.140 of the Constitution, applying art.137(5) of the earlier Weimar text.

[17] See R. Pahud de Mortagnes, 'Les Églises et l'État en Suisse en 1995', *EJCSR*, 3 (1996), p.141 at pp.143–4.

[18] See B. Primetshofer, 'Church and State in Austria 1996-1997', *EJCSR*, 4 (1997), pp.121–2.

[19] See R. Persenius, 'Church and State in Sweden', *EJCSR*, 4 (1997) p.155 at pp.157–8.

In English ecclesiastical law, even if the Church of England and its dioceses cannot be, in any normal sense, owners of property, that is not true of the corporate bodies of cathedrals, or of bishops and incumbents in their quality as corporations sole. If one had to envisage a disestablished Church of England, its nature would be better reflected in a new, special legal entity which would enable this holding of property by individual office-holders rather than by sweeping up all ecclesiastical property into one gigantic trust.

There seems to be a general recognition in the various legal systems of Europe that a minister of religion is not an employee but an office-holder.[20] The terms upon which ministers hold office, their security of tenure, is generally left to the internal rules of the church in question; in the Scandinavian countries, dismissal is often reserved to the state.

Financial Assistance for the Churches

There is no direct statistical correlation between the constitutional status of a church and the degree of financial assistance it receives from the state.[21] The Orthodox Church in Greece enjoys very large state subsidies, the Church of England virtually none except in respect of the repair of its historic buildings. Elsewhere many different practices are to be found. The German 'church tax' is amongst the best known, being collected by the revenue authorities on behalf of the churches. Spain and Italy have a related system, under which (taking Italy as the example) 0.8 per cent of an individual taxpayer's assessment is distributed, according to the taxpayer's directions in his tax return, to one of the participating churches (those which have signed an agreement with the state; not all choose to do so).

In other countries, such as Belgium and Luxembourg, the state pays the stipends and pension costs of the clergy and of some lay employees. The same is true in Alsace-Moselle in respect of the ministers of the 'recognized churches', as part of a system pre-served from the period of German administration of that region,

[20] The issue determined by the Court of Appeal in *Coker v Diocese of South-wark* (July 1997).

[21] See D. McClean 'State Finance for European Churches', *Ecclesiastical Law Journal*, 2 (1991), p.116.

one of the few parts of France with a large Protestant population.[22] In the rest of France, the *laïcité* of the Republic is better preserved, but a feature of the separation of church and state in 1905 was that all church buildings existing at that date became the property of, and are maintained by, the local *commune*. As any visitor to France soon discovers, the standard of maintenance varies markedly from place to place, but what could be seen as wholesale expropriation has in the event relieved the Roman Catholic Church in France of a major financial responsibility.

Educational and Chaplaincy Work

This is not the place to essay a comparative study of European educational systems and the churches' involvement in them.[23] It is, however, significant how 'live' and sensitive an issue is the place of the churches and of religious education in schools. This is another area in which different national histories create quite different contexts. For example, until recent years a primary school teacher in Greece had to be a member of the Orthodox Church because the curriculum included religious education in accordance with the tenets of that church. The long involvement of the churches in the provision and governance of education in England makes for a relationship within which legislative provision for a daily act of worship is acceptable. In sharp contrast, the famous decision of the Federal Constitutional Court of Germany in May 1995 on the unconstitutionality of a Bavarian schools regulation requiring a crucifix on the wall of each classroom sparked a major debate. So did the question of the reintroduction of religious education in the schools of the former German Democratic Republic after reunification; one *Land* (that of Brandenburg) opted for a subject called 'Life, Ethics and Religion'.[24] In France, where the churches appoint teachers of religious education through the institution of *aumônerie*,

[22] See F. Messner, 'Le Droit local cultuel Alsacien-Mosellan en 1995', *EJCSR*, 3 (1996), p.53.

[23] For a study of the position in 1989, see a volume by the European Consortium for Church–State Research, *Church and State in Europe: State Financial Support, Religion and the School* (Milan, 1992). See also much interesting comparative material in C. Hamilton, *Family, Law and Religion* (London, 1995).

[24] For these developments, see J. Listl, 'The Development of Civil Ecclesiastical Law in the Federal Republic of Germany 1995/1996', *EJCSR*, 3 (1996), pp.13–15.

a proposal to change the day upon which such classes were held provoked much public debate.

The participation of the churches in chaplaincy work in hospitals, penal establishments and the armed forces is, it seems, relatively unproblematic.

Equality?

An issue lurking uncomfortably behind a number of these topics is that of equality or inequality as between the churches. Some would argue that freedom of religion, fully understood, precludes any structural inequality between the various churches or faiths. There will almost always be inequality in numbers, and often in the historical significance of a church, and it is these factors rather than any legal provision which, for example, gives the Roman Catholic Church a special position in Ireland.

There can be said to be marked inequality in countries with an 'established' church: Denmark, England, Finland, Greece, Scotland, and Sweden. In Austria, Italy, Portugal and Spain, the system of concordats with the Catholic Church, instruments having a special status because of the international legal personality of the Holy See, gives a privileged position to that church, although parallel agreements with non-Catholic churches are going some way towards correcting the most glaring aspects of the resulting discrimination. In Belgium, Germany, Luxembourg, and in Alsace-Moselle, there are significant financial advantages for designated churches, though these are not restricted to any one single church. In Switzerland, there are as many systems of church–state relations as there are cantons. By a process of elimination, we appear to be left with the Republic of Ireland[25] and the Netherlands as countries in which the state can lay convincing claim to religious neutrality.

The Nature of the Debate

A reader hoping that this essay might present a neat balance-sheet in terms of 'establishment' and 'disestablishment' will have been

[25] And Northern Ireland; and possibly Wales.

disappointed. The issues are much more complex and can interact in unexpected ways.[26] There is an odd sense, too, in which the legal position can be out of step with aspects of actual practice. The Netherlands has been cited as scoring high in terms of religious neutrality, but its coins are inscribed *God met ons* (just as the separation of church and state in the United States coexists with the inscription 'In God We Trust').

The only conclusion which is offered is that the terms of the debate should recognize the reality of the continuing relationship between church and state in this as in every other country. The question is how best to express that relationship, given a particular history and legal tradition. While not underestimating the importance of symbolism and ceremony, not least in a constitutional monarchy, we need to bear in mind that the relationship also finds expression in school classrooms, hospitals and prisons; at weddings and funerals; in the joys and sorrows of a nation.

It will be clear that a ringing call for disestablishment, for a complete separation of church and state, would actually leave many questions unanswered. Is it a call for a system on the French model, with almost all the cost of church repairs borne by local authorities; and with no question of value added tax being payable? Does it involve a review of who provides, and who pays for, religious education? Would the churches' ministry in old people's homes be paid for as is hospital chaplaincy?

These are administrative and legal questions. A lawyer contributing an essay in honour of a bishop (even a canonist-bishop) must end by asserting the primacy of pastoral, spiritual and mission issues, which ecclesiastical law must serve.

---

[26] See *Campaign to Separate Church and State Ltd v Minister for Education* [1996] 2 ILRM 241 (Irish High Court) (State support for denominationally controlled schools with chaplains held consistent with constitutional bar on the endowment of religion as no discrimination between churches involved).

Notes on Contributors

Gerald Bray read classics at McGill University (Montreal) and at the Sorbonne before completing his theological studies at Cambridge. He was ordained in the Diocese of Chelmsford in 1978 and taught Christian doctrine at Oak Hill College (London) from 1980 to 1992. Since then he has been Anglican Professor of Divinity at Beeson Divinity School, Samford University (Birmingham, Alabama, USA). He speaks nine languages fluently (including Greek and Russian) and is the editor of the Anglican journal *Churchman*. He has written several books, including most recently *The Doctrine of God* (1993), *Documents of the English Reformation* (1994), *Biblical Interpretation, Past and Present* (1996) and *The Anglican Canons 1529–1947* (1998). He is currently preparing an edition, translation and commentary of the Henrician canons of 1535 and the *Reformatio Legum Ecclesiasticarum*.

Rupert Bursell QC, LL B, MA, D.Phil. is one of Her Majesty's Circuit Judges and a Clerk in Holy Orders. He is Chancellor of the Dioceses of Durham and St Albans, Deputy Chancellor of the Diocese of York and formerly Chancellor of the Diocese of Bath and Wells. He is a regular contributor to the *Ecclesiastical Law Journal* and author of *Liturgy, Order and the Law* (Oxford, 1996).

Norman Doe, born in the Rhondda, studied law at University College, Cardiff, and Magdalene College, Cambridge, and theology at St Michael's College, Llandaff. A barrister (Middle Temple), he has taught at Cambridge, Essex, Nantes and Poitiers, and is a senior lecturer at Cardiff Law School, Director of the LL M in Canon Law and Director of the Centre for Law and Religion. An honorary member of the senior common room at Magdalen College, Oxford (1996–7) and visiting fellow at Pusey House (1997), he is author of *Fundamental Authority in Late Medieval English Law* (Cambridge, 1990), *The Legal Framework of the Church of England* (Oxford, 1996), and *Canon Law in the Anglican Communion* (Oxford, 1998), editor of *Essays in Canon Law* (Cardiff, 1992), and organist at St Edward's Church, Cardiff.

Gillian Evans, D.Litt. (Oxford), Litt.D. (Cambridge), FRHistS, FRSA, British Academy Research Reader in Theology (1986–8), lectures in history and theology in Cambridge. She was a member of the Archbishops' Group on the Episcopate and of the Faith and Order Advisory Group of the Church of England General Synod (1986–96). She is a member of English ARC. Her publications include a series of books on medieval authors and an ecumenical trilogy, *Problems of Authority in the Reformation Debates* (1992), *The Church and the Churches* (1994) and *Method in Ecumenical Theology* (1996). She is the author of *Discipline and Justice in the Church of England* (1998).

Brian Ferme is a priest of the Diocese of Portsmouth, with a D.Phil. from Oxford and a pontifical doctorate in canon law. He is at present Professor of Canon Law at the Gregorian University (Rome), and a visiting Professor at the Lateran University. He has published a book on Lyndwood (1996), various articles on the history of canon law, and most recently an introduction to the history of canon law from the beginnings to Gratian. He is a Fellow of the Royal Historical Society.

David Harte read law at Trinity Hall, Cambridge, graduating in 1966. After being called to the Bar at Gray's Inn he practised in common law chambers in Newcastle upon Tyne, teaching criminal law part-time at Durham University. He took the Diploma in Criminal Law at Cambridge as a member of Corpus Christi College. He is now a senior lecturer at Newcastle Law School in the University of Newcastle and practises part-time at the Bar. He specializes in environmental law with a particular interest in the conservation of churches and other historic buildings. He obtained the LL M in Canon Law at Cardiff in 1996 and is developing undergraduate teaching at Newcastle in law and religion. A significant aspect of this is the legal treatment of religion in schools. He is a reader in the Diocese of Newcastle, licensed to St Nicholas' Cathedral and is a member of the editorial committee of the *Ecclesiastical Law Journal*.

Richard Helmholz is Ruth Wyatt Rosenson Professor of Law at the University of Chicago. He is a graduate of Princeton University and Harvard Law School and he also received a Ph.D. in medieval history from the University of California, Berkeley, in 1970. He is a Fellow of the American Academy of Arts and Sciences. He received a Research Prize in 1992 from the Alexander von Humboldt Foundation. His most recent book is *The Spirit of the Classical Canon Law* (University of Georgia Press, 1997).

Christopher Hill was ordained in 1969 in Lichfield Cathedral. After two curacies in that diocese he worked for fifteen years as an ecumenist, including the Anglican Co-Secretaryship of ARCIC I and II, in the service of three Archbishops of Canterbury. This was followed by a further six years as Canon Precentor of St Paul's Cathedral. In 1996 he was consecrated (Area) Bishop of Stafford, returning to the Diocese of Lichfield. He is the author of sundry miscellaneous ecumenical articles and co-editor with Edward Yarnold SJ of *Anglican and Roman Catholics: The Search for Unity; The ARCIC Documents and their Reception* (1994); and *Anglican Orders: The Documents in the Debate* (1997). He is currently vice-chairman of the Ecclesiastical Law Society.

Mark Hill is a practising barrister with a master's degree in Canon Law. He has written and lectured extensively on the laws of the Church of England and is presently engaged in preparing a second edition of his major text *Ecclesiastical Law* (London, 1995). A visiting tutor at the Inns of Court School of Law since 1989, he was elected visiting fellow of Emmanuel College, Cambridge, in 1998. He is Deputy Chancellor of the Diocese of Winchester, a member of the General Synod's Legal Aid Commission, case notes editor of the *Ecclesiastical Law Journal* and a member of its editorial board. He attends St Anne's Church, Soho, which he has served variously as churchwarden and pantomime dame.

David McClean, CBE, QC, DCL, is Professor of Law in the University of Sheffield, with particular interests in private international law and air law. A former chairman of the House of Laity of the General Synod, he serves as chairman of its Legal Advisory Commission and is Chancellor of the Dioceses of Newcastle and Sheffield. He is a member, and former president, of the European Consortium for Church-State Research.

Robert Ombres, OP, born in Italy, read law at the Universities of Bristol and London and was called to the Bar (Inner Temple). As a Dominican friar, he was ordained priest in 1976. Having studied theology at Blackfriars, Oxford, and canon law in Rome, he is now a teaching member of Oxford University's theology faculty. He has published widely, and was the promoter of justice ('devil's advocate') in the cause of canonization of Cardinal John Henry Newman.

Thomas Glyn Watkin is Director of the Centre for Contemporary Civil Law Studies and a senior lecturer at Cardiff Law School. As well as having written numerous articles on English and European legal history, Roman law and canon law, he is the author of *The Nature of Law* (Amsterdam, 1980) and *The Italian Legal Tradition* (London, 1997), and the editor of *Legal Record and Historical Reality* (London, 1989) and *The Europeanisation of Law* (London, 1998). His *Historical Introduction to Modern Civil Law* will appear in 1999. He has been a guest lecturer and visiting Professor at the Universities of Pavia and Parma in Italy, Oviedo in Spain, Münster in Germany, and Surugadai and Niigata in Japan. An ordained priest of the Church in Wales, he has been Legal Assistant to its Governing Body since 1981.

Subscribers

The following have associated themselves with the publication of this volume through subscription:

Revd M. R. Ainsworth, Worsley, Manchester
R. M. Armstrong, QC, Melbourne, Australia
Canon Peter Atkinson, Chichester
Professor J. H. Baker, QC, Cambridge
Paul Barber, London
Revd T. R. Barker, Spalding
Margaret R. Barlow, Rotherham
Peter F. B. Beesley, London
James Behrens, London
Jonathan Bell, London
Revd Paul J. Benfield, Pulborough, West Sussex
Christina Bennett, Henfield, West Sussex
J. G. Bentley, Alderney
Canon Dr Hinton Bird, Isle of Man
Revd P. E. Blagdon-Gamlen, Kettering
Desmond Bloom-Davis, Appleshaw, Hampshire
James Bonney, QC, London
Canon P. H. Boulton, Holmes Chapel, Cheshire
G. J. Bowtle, Wareham
The Venerable J. Michael Brotherton, Chichester
Roger L. Brown, Welshpool
Colin Buchanan, Bishop of Woolwich
The Venerable John Burgess, Bradford on Avon

Martin Burr, London
J. C. Burrows, Elston
R. D. H. Bursell, Winscombe, Somerset
Dr A. J. Cameron
Revd Robert Charles, Budleigh Salterton
O. W. H. Clark, Hampton, Middlesex
Messrs Claytons, St Albans
Revd Canon Paul Colton, Dublin
His Honour Judge T. A. C. Coningsby, QC, Chipstead, Surrey
Karen Counsell, Cowbridge
Clyde Croft, Geelong, Australia
Jonathan Cryer, Bishop Auckland, Co. Durham
Theodore Davey, London
Revd R. Paul Davies, St Davids
Peter Langdon Davis, Bridgend
Mark Davys, Little Haywood, Stafford
Edward James Eric Doe, Cardiff
T. C. Dutton, London
Chancellor Quentin Edwards, London
The Bishop of Exeter
S. J. A. Eyre, Kenilworth
Clare Faulds, Isle of Man
Revd David R. Felix, Runcorn
Helen S. Fields, Winchester
The Venerable William Filby, Horsham
M. J. Follett, Truro
Chancellor Norman Francis, Cardiff
Paul E. Fulford, Eastbourne
Gerald Funnell, Hastings
I. H. Garden, Ormskirk
Justin Gau, London
Chancellor Charles George, QC, Southwark
The Venerable Granville Gibson, Bishop Auckland, Co. Durham
Canon W. N. C. Girard, Balsham, Cambridge
Chancellor Michael Goodman, London
Revd Dr Mark N. Gretason, Worcester
Andrew Grime, Culcheth, Warrington
The Bishop of Guildford

Revd Barry G. Hall, Ingatestone, Essex
David Hands, QC, Kings Lynn
John Hanks, Oxford
Brian Hanson, London
P. A. Hardingham, Little Houghton, Northampton
Chancellor J. M. Harley, North Adelaide, South Australia
G. T. Harrap, Winchester
Revd Canon J. M. Haselock, Norwich
The Venerable David Hawtin, Southwell, Nottinghamshire
Paul Hedley-Saunders, Horsham
Francis Helminski, Minnesota, USA
Raymond Hemingray, Peterborough
Jonathan James Hill, Berinsfield, Oxfordshire
John Hind, Bishop of Gibraltar in Europe
Chancellor J. L. O. Holden, Burnley
Peter Edward Holden, Stalybridge
Susan Holmes, Carlisle
David John Hooson, St Asaph
Revd Patrick Irwin, Hameln, Germany
Dafydd Jenkins, Aberystwyth
Michael S. Johnson, Bury
Nigel I. Johnson, London
S. M. S. Jones, London
The Venerable T. Hughie Jones, Melton Mowbray
The Venerable Trevor Jones, Stapleford, Hertfordshire
Andrew Jordan, London
Bishop John Jukes, West Malling
Prebendary Neville Kent, Weston-Super-Mare
Fr Fergus Kerr, Blackfriars, Edinburgh
Fr Steven Kirk, Port Talbot
Sir Alister Kneller, Chichester
The Venerable G. P. Knowles, Fareham
D. G. Lambert, Llandaff
David J. Lamming, London
Dalby Landen, Reading
Lynne Leeder, London
John Graham Llewellyn, Stoke-on-Trent
Jane Logan, Lincoln

Dr E. A. Livingstone, Oxford
F. Donald Logan, Brookline, MA, USA
Revd John Masding, Bristol
The late The Rt. Revd B. J. Masters, Bishop of Edmonton
Simon M. Maybee, Bracknell
Professor Henry Mayr-Harting, Oxford
Alan K. McAllester, Chester
Major N. J. Mercer, Bielefeld, Germany
Professor Dr John Warwick Montgomery, Lidlington, Bedfordshire
Bishop C. Murphy-O'Connor, Pulborough, West Sussex
Charles Mynors, London
R. Rodney V. Nicholson, Newcastle upon Tyne
The Very Revd Michael O'Connor, Faversham
Dorothy M. Owen, Horncastle
Sir John Owen, Shipston-on-Stour
Revd Jeremy Paisey, Buckie, Banffshire
Venerable B. H. Partington, Douglas, Isle of Man
James Patrick, Bristol
Fr Kristian Paver, London
C. C. Augur Pearce, Cambridge
Revd Dr Stephen Pix, Oxford
Dr Colin Podmore, London
Nicholas le Poidevin, London
John Pope, Hailsham
The Bishop of Portsmouth
Chancellor Philip Price, QC, Cardiff
Dr John Quaife, Etchingham, Sussex
Revd Gordon F. Read, Ingatestone, Essex
The Bishop of Reading
Revd John Rees, Oxford
Frank Robson, Oxford
The Rt. Revd Dr Geoffrey Rowell, Bishop of Basingstoke
Bishop David Say
Revd M. W. Searle, York
The Rt. Revd M. C. Scott-Joynt, Bishop of Winchester
The Rt. Revd Dr John Sentamu, Bishop of Stepney
Monsignor Gerard Sheehy, Dublin
Revd Dr Jeremy Sheehy, Oxford

Revd D. J. Sherwood, Harrow
The Venerable D. J. Smith, Moreton-in-Marsh
Dr P. M. Smith, Exeter
Revd W. Becket Soule, Cambridge
Sir Richard Southern, Oxford
The Venerable Ian T. Stanes, Leicester
Simon Stokes, London
The Venerable E. C. F. Stroud, Benfleet
Moira E. B. Sutton, Swansea
Nicholas D. W. Thomas, Wirral
Revd Stephen Trott, Boughton
The Revd Prebendary Patrick Tuft, London
The Rt. Revd Dr David Tustin, Bishop of Grimsby
The late Revd Michael R. Vasey, Durham
Lionel Wadeson, Richmond, Surrey
Revd Alan Walker, London
T. M. Ll. Walters, Loughborough
The Venerable Geoffrey Walton, Wimborne
Fr Michael Wells, Brighton
The Venerable Roderick J. Wells, Lincoln
Stephen White, Cardiff
Revd Paul S. Williamson, Hanworth
David Willink, London
Canon Michael Wilson, Leicester
The Venerable Arnold Wood, Liskeard
Cliff and Sally Woolley, London
Hans van de Wouw, Honiton
Lindsay Yates, Witney
Br Philippe Yates, Canterbury
Revd Richard Yeo, Bath

Blackfriars, Oxford
Campion Hall, Oxford
Codrington Library, All Souls College, Oxford
Emmanuel College, Cambridge
Exeter College, Oxford
Lincoln Cathedral Library

Magdalen College, Oxford
Magdalene College, Cambridge
The Dean and Chapter Library, Norwich Cathedral
The Principal and Chapter, Pusey House, Oxford
The Library, Ripon College, Cuddesdon
The Library, Rochester Cathedral
The Library, St John's College, Durham
The Library, University of Wales, Cardiff
Westminster Metropolitan Tribunal, London
The Dean and Chapter of York

Index